ADVANCE PRAISE FOR

BEING ON THE WING

Book Two in the Enneagram in Nature series, Being on the Wing: Feathered Reflections of the Enneagram Subtypes, *will appeal to readers who love birds, philosophy, and Enneagram typology.... [This] heady experience defies pat categorization or psychological perspective as it navigates the world of birds in a novel manner ... [applying] Enneagram concepts to exploring different birder types. But what sets Rosenberg's approach apart from the typical book on birds and the art of birding is its psychological associations between personalities and birding choices, which marry philosophical with psychological insights to cement a better understanding of bird and birder. Widely inviting and uplifting,* Being on the Wing *is a top recommendation for not just libraries, but discussion groups ranging from book clubs to birders and psychology gatherings who will be interested in Rosenberg's lively, unique connection between personalities, birds, and life approaches.* —Diane Donovan, Senior Editor, Midwest Book Review

Loved it! Being on the Wing *is a rare find. It blends wisdom, beauty, and playfulness into an unforgettable journey of self-discovery.... [This] delightful and informative read offers valuable insights into self-awareness, encourages personal growth, and fosters an appreciation for both human and avian nature. Even without a deep knowledge of the Enneagram, readers can enjoy this book for its engaging stories.* —C.E. Flores, Reedsy Reviews

How can an understanding of your Enneagram type lead to the discovery of who you really are? Find out in Being on the Wing, *a fascinating tour of human and bird personalities. . . . [Learn] more about your true self than you ever thought possible. There is much wisdom within these many pages.* —Doug Tallamy, entomologist, ecologist, and conservationist, author of *Bringing Nature Home* and other books

Author Angela Rosenberg's succinct yet in-depth descriptions of the nine Enneagram types come alive with texture and color, allowing readers to receive new insights into the complexities of the types [and] deepening our understanding of humanity's unique perspectives. —Sandra Smith, CET, author of *The Enneagram Map to Your Deeper Self*, and co-host of the podcast Heart of the Enneagram.

Angela Rosenberg's Being on the Wing: Feathered Reflections of the Enneagram Subtypes will help you appreciate [and] understand your personality type.... People and birds are both on epic journeys. This book can help you take flight with our winged companions. —Bill Davison, Easy by Nature podcast and newsletter

Where Nine Perfect Petals helped us understand who we are, our core characteristics, strengths, and weaknesses based on the Enneagram personality typology, Being on the Wing expands on this flowerbed to our subtypes . . . and the nuances in approaching our opportunities for growth. —Sadye Páez, PhD, MSPT, MPH, Science Communications Director, Vertebrate Genomes Project

Both informative and entertaining, Angela Rosenberg's second book, Being on the Wing, is a delightful read. The author weaves the threads of reflections on life, observations of people's interactions with one another, and the wonder of bird behavior into an unexpected and beautiful tapestry. One cannot help but ponder what our feathered friends might teach us if we are open to the possibility that we can learn by looking at things another way. Dr. Rosenberg's rather tongue-in-cheek (or should I say, beak?), self-deprecating style is engaging and integral to the book's charm and whimsical approach. Enhanced by colorful and accurate images, this book is the perfect addition to anyone's coffee or patio table. —Jennifer Collins, author of the Love That Does Not Die trilogy.

BEING ON THE WING

FEATHERED REFLECTIONS ON THE ENNEAGRAM SUBTYPES

ANGELA McCAFFREY ROSENBERG

Book Two in the Enneagram in Nature Series

To my father, Joseph "Mac" McCaffrey

Who opened my eyes, ears, and heart to the wonder of birds

CONTENTS

To know a bird, you have to become a bird, and to become a bird, you have to enter the bird. You have to enter the bird to know what the bird knows. You have to shift your shape to understand ancient bird philosophy. To know a bird, to really know a bird, you have to embrace what the bird knows. When you do, then you are free.

Frank Inzan Owen

PART I
A LOVE OF BIRDS

THE TAO OF BIRDS AND CATS

FIRST: THAT DAMN CAT.

I would not be surprised if my first uttered words as a baby were "damn cat"; and until I uncover my baby book, likely long lost, I'm going to assume that was the case. As a child I heard that phrase yelled out by my exasperated father, "Mac," multiple times daily from the day I was brought home from the hospital. Now, to clear his record, I need you to know that my dad was not a "cussing man"; all the more reason for this oft hollered expletive to remain a strong memory. Nor do I believe that my father was a cat-hater. In truth, my dad loved all animals. And I believe what my dad had, first and foremost, was a fondness for birds, and about the only traits birds and cats hold in common is being on opposite ends of the prey-predator spectrum.

Even stronger than my auditory memory of *damn cat* is the sound of my father whistling the tune of the woodland bird, the bobwhite; also his sweet rendering of the call of the whippoorwill on long, hot, summer nights in Jackson, Mississippi. I was raised with birds and shared Dad's love of them.

Ironically, it was shortly before my first birding trip to Costa Rica when I had my first pivotal cat experience. It began with a small cat sitting underneath our old, reliable tractor the day before we left town. My initial response (did I say, *mistake?*) was to exclaim to my husband that I had spotted a kitty by the tractor. And he, being practical said, "Whatever you do, don't feed that kitty or we will end up with a cat that we do not want!"

Well, that ship had sailed, as I am an indisputable Enneagram Type Two, and thus had already deposited a bowl of milk next to the tractor. As I removed the empty bowl from the yard, I was a bit sad because I assumed that, while we were traveling, *our* kitty would move on to other, more generous farms. My husband's last words as we departed for the airport were, "If the kitty is here when we return, she is *meant to be.*"

My first cat, "Meant to Be" was waiting by the back door ten days later, and "Minty" lived with us for twelve wonderful years. I guess birds and cats do have a way of merging if the heart is in the right place. In many moments on that birding trip I guiltily thought of "my kitty" back home—and I contemplated if I could possibly love a cat. Now, two cats in, I no longer ponder this thought, but I do reflect upon the vastness and wonder of nature and of the many lessons it has yet to teach me about my relationship with all creatures.

It is this pondering that led me to explore the relationship of nature to the Enneagram.

For those of you who read the first book in this series, *Nine Perfect Petals: The Enneagram for Flower Gardeners,* you may recall that I began with a quote by George Bernard Shaw: *The best place to find God is in a garden. You can dig for him there.* The resonance of that quote is that I have often found the divine through the soil, with my hands in the dirt. In this book, I will humbly stay grounded as I lift my eyes to the sky for inspiration.

Thankfully, I did not inherit a familial aversion of cats. However, I *am* grateful that I did inherit my father's love of birds. And in case we ever meet, I did not acquire the whistling gene. I can't whistle a bird song to save my life. But the good news is that I'm living in the twenty-first century and there's an app for that failing.

YOUR STORY

What is the story you are working on
that doesn't have an ending yet?
Laurie Patton

If you're reading this book, I'm willing to bet you share my love of birds. But I'm also writing about the Enneagram, which will help you reflect on *your own story*. As you contemplate your life-chapters—embedded with times of awakening and resilience, heartache and joy—the Enneagram typology will illuminate scenes and characters. It will shed light on the narratives and perspectives constantly unfolding around you. It will awaken you to elements that may consciously or unconsciously inhabit your "back story" and provide insight and direction to transform your story moving forward.

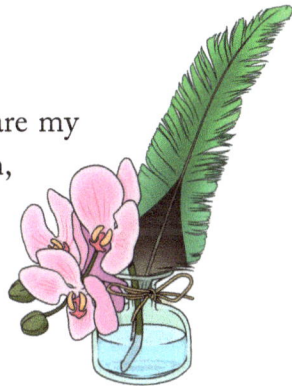

Barbara Brown Taylor, in her book *Holy Envy*, writes, "As natural as it may be to try to translate everything into my own (religious) language, I miss a lot when I persist in reducing everything to my own frame of reference." What insight she has in sharing this perspective. In this vein she posits one of life's fundamental questions: "Should we not all be continually asking ourselves, 'What am I missing'?" Or perhaps, my own daily revelation, *Crap! Look what I missed!*

Enneagram wisdom posits that we have daily *choices* that, if made, will foster healthier relationships and resourcefulness. Like the Sankofa,[1] a symbolic bird with its feet firmly planted forward while its head turns backwards to reach an egg, in various stages throughout life we find ourselves looking to the past for clues to aid us in moving forward. Our past experiences can serve to enlighten and inform, as well as caution and warn us.

---

1 Sankofa is a Twi word from the Akan Tribe of Ghana, Africa, from a proverb translated as "It is not taboo to go back for what you left behind."

As we navigate these times, I conjecture that we are more like the birds than we realize. As birds migrate they encounter natural elements that are out of their control—gale-force winds and pelting rains. Are we not much the same, navigating difficult situations, hoping to ultimately alight on wisdom, contentment, and happiness? Would it not behoove us to navigate these times using the wisdom and lessons from our "flock"? Richard Rohr, a scholar of the Enneagram, expressed this sentiment with an eye to the sky when he shared, "We are all of us pointing toward the same moon, yet we persist in arguing about who has the best finger." What a poignant reminder to consider that there are many routes to find well-being, and we need to honor the "light" that gets us through our darkest nights.

THE ENNEAGRAM AT THE BIRD FEEDER

According to Enneagram theory, there are nine personality types, each a manifestation of one of the essential characteristics of the divine. Together they represent the complete unity and fullness of humankind; and as I will suggest in these pages, to our relationships with our feathered friends.

In the following nine chapters, you will come to know and appreciate the nine Enneagram Types, and the twenty-seven Subtypes—appreciating a bird's-eye view of Type characteristics, strengths, and challenges through feathered reflections. We will explore each Enneagram Subtype as a way to gain greater clarity—in bird parlance, we will look at Type through binoculars!

Part I will present a brief description of the Enneagram and an overview of the Enneagram *Triads, Wings, and Arrows, as well as the Passions, Instincts, and Subtypes*. It concludes noting one bird as the icon for each of the Nine Types.

In Part II, each of the nine chapters will focus on the *Nine Patterns of Flight;* i.e., the nine Enneagram personality Types in the context of birds and birding. Each chapter contains the following sections:

- Type Overview
- Flock Characteristics
- That Type's Three Subtypes
- Each Subtype's Migration Flyway
- Navigation Tips

Moreover, in the Appendices, tables will provide:

- Popular Bird Idioms and Responses by Type
- Enneagram adaptation of the old English proverb, "A bird in the hand is worth two in the bush"
- Bird Songs by Type
- The KEY to the Feathered Assessment (found on pp. 35-38)

I hope that as you read about each of the *Subtypes*, with their colorful feathers and complex traits, you will come to discover the divine in nature, your fellow bird lovers, and most importantly, yourself.

You were born with wings;
why prefer to crawl through life?
Rumi

If Simorgh unveils its face to you, you will find that all the birds, be they thirty or forty or more, are but the shadows cast by that unveiling. What shadow is ever separated from its maker? Do you see? The shadow and its maker are one and the same, so get over surfaces and delve into mysteries.

Conference of the Birds[2]

Por Qué Pajaros? (Why Birds?)

Some pets are misunderstood. Let me rephrase: The *decision to choose a certain type of pet* is often misunderstood. If a friend shares with you that they have recently purchased a sugar glider (you might first ask, what *is* a sugar glider?), you would likely embrace the notion of a cuddly little marsupial as a cute, exotic pet. I will wager that you would not question a

---

2 Simorgh, a mythical, wise bird of Persia, appears in all eras of Iranian art. The Sufi poet Attar of Nishapur penned "Conference of the Birds," in which thirty or forty birds go on a journey; each bird represents a human fault which prevents humanity from attaining enlightenment.

friend's choice of a bunny, a turtle, or a fish as a pet. *However,* try sharing that you have donkeys as pets. I vividly recall a boat trip with six tourists, one a very introverted, non-English speaker. After four hours on the river, sharing stories of hobbies and pets, this woman spoke her first and only two words, directed at me: "Por qué burros?" Go ahead, just try telling someone that you own donkeys. I promise you that nine out of ten people will respond, "Donkeys? *Why donkeys?*" It is uncanny that while people can choose a flying, nocturnal glider with no consequence, a donkey as a pet seems to elicit total puzzlement. Aghast at the question, I respond that donkeys are very friendly, smart, and protective. But between you and me, *I'm not sure why we have donkeys!*

What does this have to do with the Enneagram and birds, you won-der? It seems that my sharing that I'm writing a book about the En-neagram and birds elicits a similar response: "Why *birds?*" Because birds remind us that there is a realm of nature that is beyond our immediate reach. Similar to the powers of the Enneagram, birds testify that we can migrate to embrace new ways of being, they show us that we can fly out-side of our comfort zone. Birds invite us to look at more than what meets us at eye-level; they invite us to listen and gaze upward, beyond what is, to what might be possible.

My "feathered reflections" are a compilation of personal stories, anec-dotes, and bird lore that describe aspects of the nine Enneagram Types and twenty-seven Enneagram Subtypes. The thread among these stories is birds, and with birds come feathers—be they worn by penguin, plover, or pelican. These reflections are less about choosing a specific bird for a particular Type/Subtype; rather each story was chosen to capture nuanced aspects of Type.

Admittedly, selecting narratives to capture attributes and chal-lenges for each of the twenty-seven Enneagram Subtypes was a daunt-ing endeavor. In my profession of leadership development and executive coaching, we employ multitudes of assessments to measure personality preferences and emotional and interpersonal intelligence in humans. Un-fortunately, measuring bird intelligence and intra- inter-avian preferences is considerably more complex. The study of avian motivation and relational behavior is very much in its infancy, and, to my knowledge, there has yet to be an IQ test for birds.

Most neuroscientists agree that there are multiple forms of human intelligence; emotional, analytical, and creative-spatial, to name just a few. Harvard psychologist Howard Gardner identifies eight independent types of intelligence, several of which are arguably noted in many bird species. These multiple intelligences include bodily, linguistic, musical, logical, naturalistic (sensitivity to the natural world), spatial, interpersonal, and intrapersonal. I will let readers draw their own parallels when reading my reflections. However, I suggest you consider these intelligences when you read about the Type 3 hummingbird's dance; the multi-country migration journey of our avian neighbors; the musicality of the dawn chorus; and the downright manipulative/helpful behavior of the Type 2 crow. Many researchers continue to explore avian intelligence as a capability, the ability to reason and solve puzzles and problems. While I do not claim in-depth knowledge of bird intelligence and *bird*alities, I do have knowledge of the Enneagram *person*alities, and there are many aspects of bird behavior that can be associated with Enneagram types. I welcome disagreements, but after all is written and done, this is my book!

In my first book in the Enneagram in Nature series, *Nine Perfect Petals: The Enneagram for Flower Gardeners*, I matched flowers and gardening styles to the 9 Types. In this second book in the series, I use a similar method to relate birds' characteristics and feathered reflections to each Enneagram Type. I reflect on particular impressions and attributes of various birds, share my personal feathered reflections, and refer to bird lore to represent particular behaviors, attributes, and characteristics of each of the twenty-seven Enneagram Subtypes.

For example, I perceive the flock behavior of cedar waxwings as similar to the Type 9's distinguishing tendency to merge; or the reclusive nature of the elegant trogon as similar to the Type 5's preference to keep her emotions at bay. At many junctures, I took liberties in assuming particular bird motivations as a lens to a particular Enneagram Type and Subtype.

I am convinced that the Enneagram can be applied to the avian world as well as to people. Whether a human or a bird, the essence of the Enneagram can be summed up by this poetic sentiment: *It isn't primarily what you think, or even the actions you perform, it is what you desire that predicts behavior.* I now invite you to embrace the Nine Types and twenty-seven Subtypes of the Enneagram Typology in *Being on the Wing: Feathered Reflections on the Enneagram Subtypes.*

> *Only the truth of who you are, if realized,*
> *will set you free.*
> Eckhart Tolle

Why the Enneagram? The Enneagram Typology

The Enneagram (Greek, meaning *nine points*) is a personality typology that describes nine distinct personality points, each reflecting a core, divine quality. Some Enneagram scholars suggest the diagram was inscribed in ancient texts by Sufi scribes seeking to find the truth of divine love and knowledge through a direct, personal experience of God; others believe it originated in the Middle Ages. Regardless, the typology and the descriptions of the nine personality types, with their associated characteristics, have been well recognized throughout the centuries and among various countries and cultures, with applications across myriad professional disciplines.

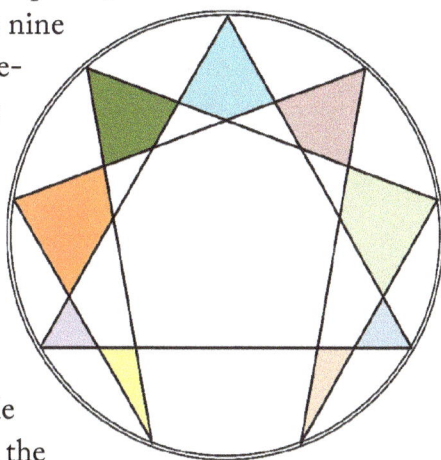

The Enneagram diagram has often been compared to a color wheel or prism, which upon exposure to white light, fans into a spectrum of basic colors. With this metaphor, every person contains all of the hues, but one particular color stands out—the specific hue of that individual. This hue equates to one of the nine Enneagram types and all of the associated characteristics of that Type—in bird vocabulary, the distinctive colors and markings of your feathers.

The Value of Typology

As a leadership coach, I am often asked questions related to the value of using personality inventories to characterize and/or differentiate individuals. This question is one that those of us using psychological profiles and assessments must constantly re-assess so that we facilitate knowledge of personality preferences and traits with intentional dignity and respect. I recall Helen Palmer, psychologist and Enneagram scholar, suggesting that we are all already ensconced in our individual boxes, and by learning the nuances of Type, we are able to see outside of our own confines; similar to removing the blinders on a horse. The fact is that we are creatures of habit, and we respond to people and events in somewhat predictable, patterned, and often compulsive ways. According to the Enneagram, these patterns are formed when we are very young, in response to a world that is complex and unpredictable.

The wisdom of the Enneagram does not label us; instead, it frees us by making a very important distinction between the core essence of who we are and the personality characteristics we routinely display. This display is defined by the Enneagram as ego—characterized by labels, masks, and judgments. Our true self, our essence, is described in terms of our genuine intentions, power, and individuality.

The ego is, though, necessary to navigating one's life; without ego we would have no core defense mechanisms! When the going is unbearable, we need a place to hide out for a while. The ego helps us cope with all of the ups and downs in life that create feelings of security and stress. Along the way, we begin to favor some values and abilities more than others. In this way, we create layer upon layer of preferred ways of perceiving, feeling, and doing. These adaptations could be likened to a peacock's increasingly heavy plumage: eventually we become grounded by the very characteristics that helped us to cope; we have buried our beautiful, core essence.

Through self-awareness, we can transcend the ego, gaining a deeper awareness of how our true motivations drive our thoughts, feelings, and resultant behaviors. On this path we gain greater agency over our lives. In turn, the Enneagram provides us with a migration map and compass to better understand others, rather than presume understanding and seek to substantiate one's assumptions.

> *Let me keep my distance, always, from those who*
> *think they have the answers. Let me keep company,*
> *always, with those who say "Look!" and laugh in*
> *astonishment, and bow their heads.*
> Mary Oliver, Excerpt from *"Mysteries, Yes"*

A Note on Labels

In the world of birds, classification is not only common, it is essential. Birding is, in essence, identifying birds, not only for personal enjoyment, but for conservation purposes. At its simplest, it is critical to identify how many birds of a certain species or family exist, and where conditions might be harmful to their survival. From a psychosocial standpoint, I would argue that the identification of human motivations and behaviors is equally essential to human survival, enabling our ability to truly know one another more deeply.

The import of why, when, and how we label occurred to me a number of years ago while on safari in Tanzania. The ultimate goal of our driver, with many years of experience, was to find what the vast majority of tourists want to see, the "big five": lion, leopard, elephant, buffalo, and rhinoceros. In contrast, the most important thing for our group of four was identifying birds, and the minute we spotted our first bee-eater, I was smitten. Upon sighting this bird we immediately implored our driver to stop, and he looked at us in mild confusion, as if we had mistakenly taken the wrong trip. He then muttered the word "ndege"; the Kiswahili term used for basically any number of flying objects, including birds and planes. It also strictly translates as "birdbrained," which may have reflected our driver's true sentiment regarding our request. What struck us was that our driver never even considered introducing us to the variety and colors of the birds around him because he had clumped us with "big animal" tourists (in his defense, most safari tourists are just that); he was doing his job. Birds, to his thinking, were non-essentials, placed in the category of everything that flies. He was hedging his bets and pointing out creatures on the land, not the sky.

To me the experience of labeling birds and calling them by name is a way of ascribing and affirming their unique and undeniable value to our planet. In knowing birds, we can track their migration and behavior, a living map to best understand and support them, especially when they are in crisis. In knowing the names and whereabouts of birds, we can better serve them: such as by turning out our night lights to assure their safe migration or creating environments of native plants so various species can survive and thrive. In return for their safety, the birds provide us with an interactive map on climate change.

I propose a similar theme for humans. By exploring the nine Types and twenty-seven Subtypes of the Enneagram one can mine deeper levels of knowing fellow human travelers, their unique motivations, and their paths to feel safe and secure. As a result of these insights, we can hope to evolve into a more compassionate community.

As you deepen your understanding of the Enneagram, you can choose to give "the most generous explanation" when human behavior is

perplexing. You can then choose to create conditions under which you and others will thrive in harmony. No matter if a friend, foe, family member, or acquaintance, the Enneagram will deepen your appreciation of how others move through the world at a different pace; occupy a different space. From my lens, this awareness is not only vital, but essential to human survival.

Birds for leaves, and leaves for birds . . .
What good is accuracy amidst the perpetual
scattering that unspools the world.

Ada Limón, from "It's the Season I Often Mistake"

The Enneagram Triads

Not unlike how the seasons of the year guide and inform bird behaviors, the Enneagram Triads are a natural place to begin our journey to gain insight from the Enneagram. Referred to by some as the three *centers of energy*, the Triads are, in my humble opinion, the best way to gain familiarity with the motivations that are the core of the Enneagram personality typology. Each of the three Triads contains three of the nine Enneagram types. The first I will describe includes Types 2-3-4; the second includes Types 5-6-7; the third includes Types 8-9-1. Various authors use key descriptors to describe each of the Triads, but for the purpose of this book, I will use the terms I feel are most relevant to the birds:

- 2-3-4s: Heart (Love Birds)
- 5-6-7s: Brain (Bird Brains)
- 8-9-1s: Gut (Big Birds)

You have surely heard the old adage, "You can't judge a book by its cover." Likewise, one shouldn't judge human personality based on behavior! Rather, by exploring our own and others' energies and *reasons why*, we can gain insight into the motivations that inspire and challenge individualized ways of feeling, thinking, and being in the world. That said, join me in exploring the Triads—three distinct approaches to life, the seasons of our personality.

> *You must take personal responsibility. You cannot change the circumstances, the seasons, or the wind, but you can change yourself. That is something you have charge of.*
>
> Jim Rohn

Heart (Lovebirds) 2-3-4s

Also known as the *relational* Triad, individuals who reside in this group appear the most emotional of all types, while in fact, they may be least in touch with their true emotions. The concept of *feeling* for these individuals is their focus on their own value. Those dwelling in this Triad are concerned with their own image and how they are viewed by others. As a result of this need, birders in this Triad will keep *doing*, embarking on the next task to validate their worth. At some level, 2-3-4s are all acting a part and are skilled at performing the role that is needed for the situation.

Types
2-3-4

Heart

(Lovebirds)

Those in this Triad are often described as *moving outward*, in that they display a need to relate and engage with others in order to relate to life. As birders, 2-3-4s will generally engage through their feelings in some way or another. A Type 2 birder will focus on sharing and helping others, forgetting that her own binoculars may need some serious adjusting.

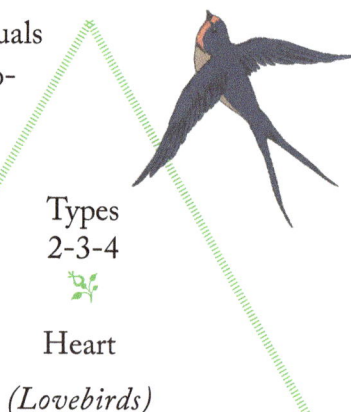

The Type 3 Birder has trouble relating to her own/others feelings and is all about trying to portray herself as accomplished. She will pursue any and every birding challenge with fervor and go to great heights to prove herself. The Type 4 Birder is so focused on pondering her own feelings that she forgets that others also experience emotional highs and lows. This birder may feel and express sheer ecstasy when sighting an exquisite bird, but reveal a sense of bird-envy when the birds she longs to view elude her.

At the end of the day, birders in this Triad trust their actions and see their birding as a task to be conquered.

Brain (Bird Brains) 5-6-7s

Also known as the *head* or *thinking* Triad, individuals who reside in this group appear wise and knowledgeable, while often feeling apprehensive.

Types
5-6-7

Brain
(Bird Brains)

No one would question being afraid to dive into a shark tank or dive off of a cliff. The turbulent ride of life definitely requires perceptive choice and a measure of instinctual caution in the face of the unknown. Fear creates watchfulness in the face of danger. Yet the key for Types 5-6-7 is to *acknowledge the fear—but not be controlled by it.* At some level, 5-6-7s are afraid that if they stop seeking information and perspective, they will never be prepared or find the answers they seek. Individuals in this Triad are often described as *holding back*, in that they display a need to step away from life and gain distance. As birders, 5-6-7s are all driven, at some level, by feeling ill-equipped for birding. This will not do in bird-land!

The 5 birder will externalize her anxiety and read or podcast on the regional birds prior to donning her binoculars. I personally think birding is the perfect hobby for the Type 5—in part because most 5s would prefer

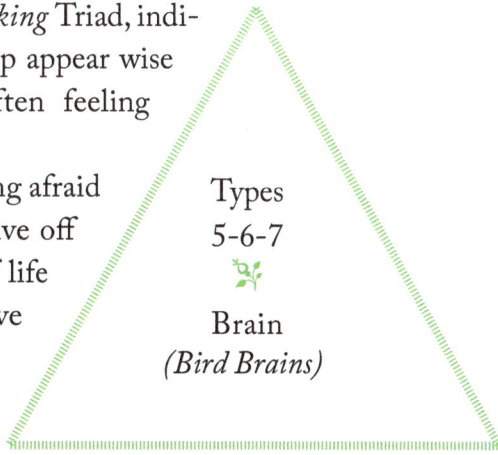

birds to humans; also because birding is an observational hobby and that is the love language of the Type 5! The 6 birder tends to internalize her anxiety and sees birding through the lens of preparation and precaution. Simply find a Type 6 to know the best viewing spots and bird habitats; but if you are looking for bird-spontaneity, find yourself a Type 7. The Type 7 birder tends to fly away from her fears by retreating into the realm of imagination to enjoy birding adventures. There is no such phrase as *the sky is the limit* for Type 7 birders.

At the end of the day, birders in this Triad trust their intellect and mental energy, viewing birds as an infinite mystery to behold.

Gut (Big Birds) 8-9-1s

Also known as the *gut* Triad, individuals who reside in this group appear to be strong and invincible, while often concealing feelings of vulnerability inside. The concept of *instinctual energy* for these individuals is to act on their gut feelings about their next birding quest. At some level, 8-9-1s are afraid that if they "let down their guard," they will lose control of themselves in one form or another. Those residing in this Triad tend to have core issues around managing anger. In that sense, instinctual types are often described as *holding their ground*, in that they display a need to be firm and express their core, instinctual energy to hold on to their sense of self.

Types 8-9-1

Gut
(Big Birds)

As birders, 8-9-1s "self-forget" in some way or another: 8 birders lust for big, rare, colorful birds. A sighting of a house wren is not on their radar unless said wren can sing in Spanish or is a rare albino wren. The 1 forgets that birding isn't about being the perfect identifier or keeping the most accurate bird-list records. Nor do their birding buds need to be informed about all that the Type 1 birder knows. The Type 9 enjoys birding at their own pace and forgets her own bird list and desired sightings, instead merging with the group agenda.

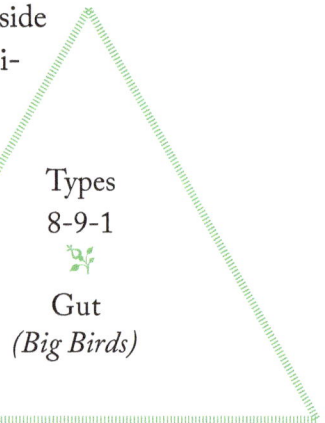

At the end of the day, individuals in this Triad trust their judgments and see birding as a conquest.

> *My turn shall also come:*
> *I sense the spreading of a wing.*
> Osip Mandelstam

Arrows and Wings

וּבְצֵל כְּנָפֶיךָ יֶחֱסָיוּן לְצֵב *B'tzel k'nafecha y'chesayun*
In the shadow of
Your wings, we find shelter.
Psalm 57:1

When asked about the quote above, Rav Kook, an influential Jewish poet, scholar, and spiritual leader responded that this Psalm is to remind us that even in times of darkness a divine presence is with us, and there is ascension towards light. I am in awe of birds' migratory journeys by the light of the moon, the embodiment of our opportunity to migrate through our own darkness and burdensome patterns, toward a place of safety and security; to fly through the storm clouds to eventual lightness of being.

The Enneagram, at its core, reflects a spiritual journey; it provides wisdom related to how to *navigate toward the light* rather than being victims to our own egos and passions—the Enneagram offers us *a pair of sturdy wings*.

The detailed Enneagram diagram (opposite) illustrates that each number has a line that connects the Type with four other numbers, one on each side, called *Wings*, and the other two connected via *Arrows*. The specific numbers that are connected to a particular Type are associated with characteristics that provide opportunities for growth. While your core Type/number will never change, these other four Types/numbers provide the direction and opportunity to flourish and become more resourceful.

Sadness flies away
on the wings of time.
Jean de La Fontaine

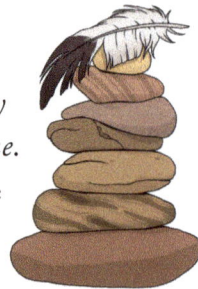

Migrating with the Arrows (Flyways)

The Arrows of the Enneagram are, in large part, what allow the Enneagram to guide us and make this particular typology so profound. While there are countless personality assessments that tell us who we *are*, the Enneagram Arrows point us toward the qualities to which we might *aspire*—to be a resourceful, more resilient version of ourselves. Equally, if not more importantly, the Enneagram Arrows provide insight into when we have lost our way and point us in the direction to regain a balance in our lives. In this sense, the Enneagram typology is a *personality navigation map* that allows an individual to expand her repertoire of behavior in new and dynamic directions. In this book, in deference to the parlance of birds, we will call the Arrows, *flyways*.

Thousands of birds migrate en masse each year beginning in late summer through the fall, embarking upon a long, often harsh, exhausting journey. This instinctual call to warmer climates is a flight toward security, to a place of safety. *Flyways* are the paths used by large numbers of birds while migrating between their breeding grounds and their overwintering quarters. Notably, flyways describe broad, generalized pathways; they are

Peaceful
Egret
9

Powerful 8   1 Conscientious
Penguin   Cardinal

Joyful 7   2 Supportive
Pelican   Bluebird

Vigilant 6   3 Accomplished
Killdeer   Hummingbird

Observant 5   4 Aesthetic
Owl   Great Blue Heron

not rigid or narrowly defined routes. Depending upon their geographical start point and what they need to thrive, particular birds will choose a specific flyway.

Similar to the birds, we will explore the Enneagram Arrows, our flyways, as a means to move away from our core Enneagram Type, our psychosocially safe-home, to migrate and adopt the resilient behaviors of another Type. In the bird world, this migration is vital because the earth literally tips on its axis, resulting in profound seasonal changes. Yet, profound changes occur in our human existence as well, when for unforeseen reasons, our personal world *feels* like it turns upside down. At these times, not unlike the birds, our ability to migrate using flyways—to change course—can actually *save us from our un-resourceful selves*. Resisting our less than optimal idiosyncratic behaviors and our well-trodden, ego-layered responses, we can migrate in the direction of the Arrows/flyways to garner resources from other Enneagram points.

I once read: "It is in migration that birds can truly stagger us" (*Living Bird*, p. 50). Envision a wee, ruby-throated hummingbird: this tiny creature, body mass topping out at approximately three to five grams, the weight of three or four raisins! Now picture these little guys as they take to the air and migrate (without a "smart" phone GPS) from North Carolina to Mexico. They fly facing immense natural forces such as hail, wind gusts, and sand storms. C'mon! If this li'l-hummer can migrate powered only by the immeasurable and constant beat of tiny wings; I think you can migrate, too, don't you?

And just when you thought—*These flyways are cool!*—there's an even more insightful aspect to Enneagram navigation. In general, a particular Type can follow the flyway to either connected Type to draw from the energy and characteristics of that Type. But there's a bit of a twist to the Enneagram flyway migration. When we are overly tired or on the edge, as when the squirrels are gobbling every last bit of birdseed, we are in a less secure period in life. While in this stressful state, our tendency is to migrate in the direction of the flyway pointing *away* from our core number (see diagram, p. 19). When we arrive we have an inclination to absorb and portray some of the *less beneficial* qualities of that connected Type. However, the wisdom of the Enneagram can guide us to stretch and draw from the more resourceful qualities of that Type as well.

In contrast, when we are *on the wing*, as in "The weather forecast is for *Carolina* blue skies (I have no shame! Shout out for the University of North Carolina Tarheels) and mild winds," we tend to be in a less stressful, more healthy "space" in life. In this secure space, our personality tends to move against the direction of the Arrow pointing toward our core number (see diagram, p. 19). When we move in this direction, against the Arrow, we tend to absorb and portray some of the more healthy and resourceful aspects of that connected Type when we arrive.

Lean on Your Wings

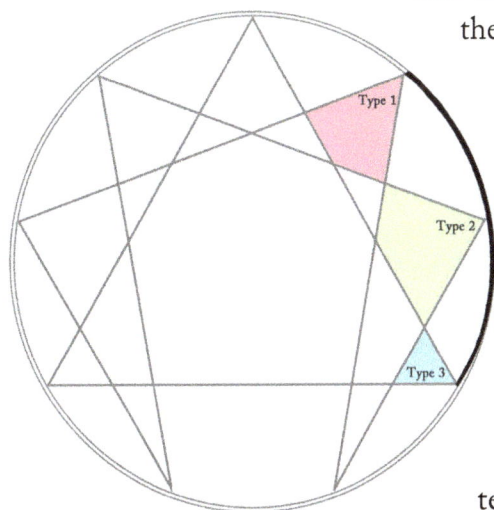

This diagram highlights the Wings of the Type 2 birder. The numbers on either side of the core number—in this case, 1 and 3—are called the *Wings* of the 2. Not unlike true Wings, these numbers provide us an opportunity to soar! On the Enneagram, characteristics of either Wing can influence our core personality Type— and we can use these characteristics to "lean (aka Wing) on" when our core personality needs some support. Similar to the Arrows/flyways, the specific numbers that scaffold the core Type provide opportunities to thrive or deteriorate.

In the avian world, one can think of the Enneagram Wings as a mechanism to keep us aloft by providing us with balance and directions. Our Wings are as essential to our core being as water is to survival.

The Enneagram Subtypes: Passion x Instinct = Subtype

Once the realization is accepted that even between the closest human beings infinite distances exist, a wonderful living side by side can grow, if they exceed in loving the distance between them which makes it possible for each to see the other whole against the sky.

Rainer Maria Rilke

The Passions

Each of the 9 Enneagram Types has a unique passion. These are emotional patterns or fixations that, while always present, are largely unconscious and drive many of our behaviors. These emotional patterns developed in early life to protect us from psychological traumas; they were necessary to maintain our sense of psychological safety and security.

It is important for one to recognize the 9 Type Enneagram passions, as they are the core of our personality's defense system. As the saying goes, the best defense is a good offense. In Enneagram parlance, in understanding our egoic emotional patterns, we have an opportunity to consciously and intentionally engage in the world with a mind to our own and others' well-being. The passions, therefore, are nothing to be ashamed of—they can be keys to our better selves.

Type 1	
Passion: Anger	The headliner for the Type 1 is the distinction between what *is* and what is *right*—the line isn't blurry. Critical of the general state of things, the feathers of this bird are often standing on end. With an eagle-eye toward improvement, the Type 1 is irritated with herself and others, unable to fully display her frustration. The pickle for this person is
Manifests as: Irritation	that being the "good person," she can't show her full annoyance; instead, she holds tension in her body. And she goes about her business of cleaning up the world. Cuz' let's face it, there will always be plenty to correct.

Type 2	
Passion: Pride	The multi-talented Steve Martin said, *A day without sunshine is like, you know, night.* And the Type 2 would suggest, *A world without Type 2s is like, you know, despondent.* The passion for this bird is an ego-driven puffing of feathers, feeling more important than reality suggests. Assuming the needs of her flock, this li'l chickadee doles out seed, acorns, and worms in order to feel better about herself. The tricky part of this is that when her giving isn't well received, her quills quickly become barbs. An unconscious cycle of self-criticism and a need to be indispensable thus begins as the Type 2's day turns to night.
Manifests as: Feeling Indispensable	

Type 3	
Passion: Deceit	Can you hear the thunderous applause as you fly high? No? The Type 3 does. This stunning bird will don or dye her feathers to match the texture and colors that others admire, despite what she might like. Feathered mimicry is her gig, and like the mockingbird, usurps the tunes of other birds. The Type 3 will assume goals if it garners her with personal success. Her false plumes carefully conceal her tired, worn feathers and molting; well, that is simply out of the perfectly altered picture.
Manifests as: False image	

Type 4	
Passion: Envy	Bigger nest, sweeter song, brighter feathers. The passion-perch for this bird is just over the fence where he peers longingly at your feathered comforts. Envy from this angle is the person constantly comparing and coming up way short. His proverbial glass is regretfully half empty as he perceives yours filled to the brim. The end result is that the Type 4 may produce a drama, yet always feel deficient in the lead role.
Manifests as: Missing out	

Type 5	
Passion: Avarice	This is not about a nest egg of stolen cash. Avarice for the Type 5 is all about the heart; one that is closed for business. Much like a squirrel hoards nuts, this person hoards knowledge and resources for fear of ending up nut-less. Disconnecting from people and emotional entanglement is the safest flight pattern, albeit necessitating the avoidance of any form of expressive intensity. The roost for this bird and individual is as far away as possible from human connection.
Manifests as: Emotional disconnection	

Type 6	
Passion: Fear	This feathered friend may be occasionally on the wing but is always on the lookout. The passion of the Type 6 is fear, which translates to a constant state of apprehension and a sense that something is wrong. Living with that sort of tension, sensing a looming cat around every single corner, means contentment is out of reach. Preparation and constant vigilance are critical—*meow*.
Manifests as: Constant vigilance	

Type 7	
Passion: Gluttony	While some birds are known to overdo when it comes to day drinking (see cedar waxwings), the passion of gluttony for the Type 7 refers to an insatiable need for stimulation: experiences, things, and people. The sky does not even come close to the limit in the imagination of this positive bird. *Limitless or Bust* would be the motto for the 7. Thus, this ego-driven passion results in over-optimism and fleeing any life experience that appears humdrum or boring. This bird lives to skydive.
Manifests as: Wanting it all	

Type 8	
Passion: Lust	Get your mind out of the gutter and back in the book. We aren't talking steamy rom-coms; we *are* talk'n intensity. You name the game, and the Type 8 is all in: food, work, exercise. Go big or go home. Lust translates to an intense and strong-willed person who is excessive in almost every aspect of life. This bird assumes a very, very high perch. A Mount Everest Bird.
Manifests as: Being excessive	

Type 9	
Passion: Sloth	If you are focused on the image of a flea-ridden, moss-covered human, you are reading the wrong book. The passion of sloth for the Type 9 bears no resemblance to laziness or Costa Rican mammals. Instead, sloth refers to the act of doing—yep, you read it, *DOING*. The catch is, not doing *every* action but the *right* action; the one that matters most to the Type 9. Routine is a form of bliss for this peaceful bird, and she will merge with the direction of the flock rather than recognize her own flight pattern. Upon observation, Type 9s adopt the agenda of others rather than attending to their own desires; and that, my friends, is the very definition of self-forgetting. Now. Where was I?
Manifests as: Self-forgetting	

Instincts

The bird is powered by its own life
and by its motivation.

A.P.J. Abdul Kalam

The Enneagram describes three centers of energy—the head, heart, and gut—and three distinct subcategories for each of the nine Types, based on whether a person has a predominant drive toward **self-preservation, social interaction** in groups, or **one-to-one** bonding. According to Claudio Naranjo, a Chilean-born psychiatrist who, with Oscar Ichazo, is thought to be a principal developer of the modern Enneagram Personality Theory, the twenty-seven Subtype descriptions offer an even more refined view of the personality types than the nine types alone.

Similar to using binoculars to accurately hone in on and identify the characteristics of a specific bird, understanding Subtypes can provide refined information to assist with uncovering a person's correct Type.

In this book, each of the nine Enneagram personality types will be described according to the three distinct Subtypes for each. These Subtypes reflect the unique characteristics of *the passion* (core motivational factor) of the Type and one of three human *instinctual drives*:

- Self-preservation,
- Social Interaction, and
- One-to-One Connection.

All three instincts operate in each of us; however, one of the three will dominate, resulting in a more nuanced reflection of our Type. We each also have a secondary instinct that supports the dominant instinct. The third instinct is the least developed—often a blind spot in our personality.

Self-preservation

And we are put on earth a little space
that we may learn to bear the beams of love.
William Blake

This instinct focuses attention and resultant behavior on themes of survival and material security as related to each specific Type. Resultant focus and behaviors may include sufficiency of resources, avoidance of danger, and a sense of control in the world. The self-preservation instinct is a biological drive directing energy toward safety and security. Many of us may have experienced this feeling at one time or another; however, when it comes to nature, the concept of self-preservation takes on a new, broadened focus.

I've never been particularly fond of the phrase "canary in a coal mine," but living in our current "climate" of change—it holds newfound relevance. Regardless of the myriad reasons why, our human and bird habitats are changing, and birds are serving a valuable role in identifying the impact on Mother Earth. The proverbial "canary in a coal mine" is now a plover in the low-country marsh, a bobwhite in a Southern forest, or the elegant trogon in a Costa Rican rainforest. Bird habitats, nesting sites, and migration patterns are powerful indicators of the health of our planet, with the presence or absence of birds being prognostic of the future of human survival—like winged Ouiji boards. We best pay rapt attention to what our bird partners are foretelling. Humans have a responsibility to ensure sufficient resources so that our avian neighbors don't merely survive, but thrive. Ultimately, bird migration reminds us that, despite our differences, we can move in a unified direction. Perhaps if we adopt a self/other preservation philosophy, we will prosper, not in spite of but because of our migratory unity.

Social Interaction

My humanity is bound up in yours,
for we can only be human together.
Desmond Tutu

This instinct focuses attention and resultant behavior on themes of belonging, recognition, and relationships in social groups as related to each specific Type. Resultant behaviors may entail position and esteem in groups, and individual power relative to others.

In the early stages of writing this book, I enjoyed a cup of tea with a friend who reflected the overall sentiment of the social instinct. She had just received news of the death of a dear friend, and as she shared stories of this man I had never meet, I felt I had missed out on meeting a remarkable person. After a time, our tears mingled with laughter. She commented that when I had arrived for our visit she had felt "so cold," and now she was filled with warmth. We pondered whether shared grief serves to warm the heart. As I prepared to go, she asked me about the focus of my book; I told her that it was about birds. Without skipping a beat she exuberantly declared, "That is what I hope to come back as in my next life—a bird!" Her explanation of this reincarnation reflected the social instinct of Enneagram typology. A life fully lived is one of a collective experience.

As she gazed out into the late afternoon marsh—she disclosed that the particular type of bird didn't matter—she longed to return to the sense of "community" that birds symbolize. She stated that she had absolutely no desire to be an eagle—as she perceives the eagle as a lonely bird. She wished to return in a flock—whether on Bird Key, a gathering and roosting place for shore birds near our Folly home, or on a wire, where all of the birds sit in a row, as if in a pub, sharing tales over pints of frothy beer. In her words, "they are happy together; I want to come back as those birds." In the days following our visit I reflected on her sentiments; I hope that I am nearby when she leaves her earthly body, to bear witness to her soaring over the reeds and tidal pools with her flock.

One-to-One Connection

The bird a nest, the spider a web, man friendship.
William Blake

The One-to-One instinct focuses attention and resultant behavior on themes of quality and status of relationships with particular individuals as related to each specific Type. Resultant behaviors may include the achievement and maintenance of relationships with important others, sexual connection, interpersonal attraction, bonding, and One-to-One connections with others.

In most cases, birds are driven by instinct, due to their need to survive and procreate. However, their seductive and diverse mating rituals, quite frankly put us humans to shame (chocolates and roses, seriously?) One only needs to watch the David Attenborough PBS documentary, *Birds of the Gods*, to understand the One-to-One instinctual drive of attraction and sexual connection in the avian world: the sensual dances, the audacious contortions, and dazzling color displays. No psilocybin or 3-D glasses required, just tune in and prepare to be enthralled.

Countertypes

Lastly, for each of the nine Enneagram types, one of the three Subtypes will be, frankly, upside-down, in that it *goes against the flow* of the main energetic direction of the passion. This Subtype is termed the "Countertype." The most illustrative of these is that of the Type 6. Type 6s are known to be, by-and-large, anxious and afraid. The Countertype of the 6 is the One-to-One Subtype: the individual who is "unafraid" and exhibits behaviors that are contrary to what are known to the Type 6. In this person, anxiety is replaced by intimidation and readiness. This is the bird that flies directly into the turbulent storm; all fight, rather than flight. Each of the nine types has a "Countertype" among their three Subtypes.

In conclusion, I want to reiterate that all individuals of a particular instinct will not necessarily exhibit similar behaviors, as it is the interaction of the instinct with the passion of a specific Type that results in twenty-seven unique Subtypes. Not unlike the unique plumage of different types of sparrows, when the passion of each Type is engaged, the nuanced Subtype colors emerge.

I wish we had all been born birds instead.
Kurt Vonnegut

WHAT TYPE BIRDER ARE YOU?

I define the term "birder" broadly as not only those who wake pre-dawn with binoculars and walking sticks at the ready by the front door; but also the person who falls asleep in the hope of identifying a rare bird in her dreams. In this book the term *birder* runs the gamut from the Type 1 birders who meticulously curate their bird list (yes, they have a list!) with a date and time stamp to the Type 4 birders who seek to hear the call of the club-winged manakin while on a year-long pilgrimage in the Colombian cloud forest. Most relevant, a birder in this book is a lover of all feathered creatures; no lists, quests, taxonomy or identifiers required.

For Fun: See Appendix III for creative lenses to use in identifying Enneagram birders.

Type 1: The Conscientious Birder

The Type 1 focuses her binoculars on improvement and is tireless in her quest to perfect herself as well as others. She is conscientious in all of her endeavors, with the highest standards in mind. Her nesting boxes, strategically placed, will meet size and entry requirements for her bird community. Her actual and metaphysical lens is trained toward conservation efforts to preserve increasingly scarce natural resources and prevent the extinction of bird species. If you notice a bird burning the midnight candle to refurbish her nest—I'd bet on a Type 1.

Consider the cardinal: If barren trees are the cold bones of winter, the startling red cardinal represents the perfect, warm, beating heart.

Type 2: The Supportive Birder

The Type 2 focuses her binoculars on "support" and is always at the ready to lend a handful of seed. She concentrates on creating a sanctuary for all comers: local and migratory. This birder will place feeders in a number of places and specific seeds to meet the dietary preferences of varied species. The Type 2 birder shares her love of birds with friends and family and wants to get "up close and personal" with her feathered buds. If you are at the vet and spot a frantic person cradling a tiny fledging wren in a hand towel, I'd lay money it's a Type 2 birder.

Consider the bluebird: If startling blue feathers lift the spirit, might a glimpse of the bluebird represent the greatest gift to humanity?

Type 3: The Accomplished Birder

If you are in search of an "accomplished" birder, train your binoculars on a Type 3, who is out to see birds; lots of birds. It is more than likely that this ambitious person will have seen the bird you saw, and have seen her raising her chicks! And bird lists? You ain't seen nothin' until you see the list of the Type 3! Absolute certainty regarding the accuracy of her identification is of less concern to the Type 3 than the quantity of sightings. She will regale you with photos of rare bird species, sharing details of the grueling hike she successfully climbed to snap said photos. Did you say you dare to compete with a Type 3? Brave birder, you be!

Consider the hummingbird: Observe a feathered sugar high when you witness the buzz, sip, dart, and dash of the smallest bird on the planet.

Type 4: The Aesthetic Birder

"Birdwatching" is a misnomer for the richness of the Type 4 birding experience, which is as much an internal as an external practice for the Type 4. She cultivates a deep spiritual and emotional communion with all things feathered. Type 4 birders long for a transcendent experience, not some mediocre bird drivel. They will find the layered meaning in birdsong, bird sightings, and bird lore. The 4 will embrace the beauty of all birds, but may envy the depth of other birders' knowledge and keen, rare sightings. While most birders *use the long lens* when photographing birds, Type 4s *long to use* the close-up lens. You may want to follow their gaze—sure to be aesthetically and emotionally pleasing.

Consider the great blue heron: The sun can now set low and my body rest, as I have witnessed her graceful, low flight, as if one with the the autumn gold marsh grasses.

Type 5: The Observant Birder

For the Type 5 birder, the mind is where their bird wisdom and depth of knowledge is carefully protected. If you are looking for an observant birder, take to the trail in the company of the discerning Type 5. Bliss for a Type 5 is being away from humans, on a quiet path, with binoculars and a bird identification book or Merlin application. Talk about heaven on earth. Birding is a cognitive science; a researched, methodical approach. The Type 5 birder *studies* birding: habitats, species, mating rituals, calls, etc., etc. If you are wondering where all of the Type 5s are hanging out? I have a hunch that a lot of them are in the woods, peering between the leaves, binoculars in hand.

Consider the owl: Seek, but you will rarely find. Now study, wait, and listen.

Type 6: The Vigilant Birder

The Type 6 is prepared for every bird-eventuality: binoculars, regional bird list and marker, bird app on phone, sunscreen (extra, of course), insect repel-lent (natural, non-toxic), granola (low sugar), first-aid kit (duh!), and emer-gency flares (okay, maybe that is a bit of an exaggeration, but not totally). Any bird outing with a Type 6 will be meticulously researched and planned because the 6 lives with an undercurrent of anxiety. The 6 birder will have consulted with a variety of bird websites, specialists, and listened to podcasts and, when feeling confident, will forge ahead—to find birds! Their motto might read: **Safety First, Then Warblers!**

Consider the killdeer: High alert and being prepared is the name of the game for any type of bird, but especially for the killdeer.

Type 7: The Joyful Birder

The Type 7 birder entices us to embrace the surround-sound of lilting music, raucous color, and delightful winged-dances; a waking dream that appears just beyond our reach. While the other eight Types use the slang phrase *that's for the birds* to denote something that just *isn't worth it*, the Type 7 declares, *if it were not* for the birds our world be—to put it bluntly—dismal. These bird dreamers want to add color to a world often mired in black-and-white thinking. The Type 7 invites us to consider that our seemingly unreachable goals are closer than we think, if we can only imagine them.

Consider the pelican: A waking dream: A beautiful beach, endless crystal blue water, and all you can eat seafood buffet.

Type 8: The Powerful Birder

Type 8 birders seek a bold and impressive birding experience. These individuals will also be quick to point out the paucity of birds on the trail or the lack of species. Type 8s lust for intensity, so any bird worth seeing will have robust colors, quirky behavior, and/or a notable song. No house wren or common sparrow for the Type 8—these birders are out to spot falcons and soaring eagles. If you want to experience "Big Birds"—find yourself behind the lens of the Type 8.

Consider the penguin: What is black and white and tough enough to be cold all over?

Type 9: The Peaceful Birder

A birding experience for the Type 9 progresses at an unhurried pace—as 9s are all about pursuing a peaceful experience. All that is required: birds, rocking chair, binoculars. That describes the perfect birdwatching day for a Type 9. In lieu of finding her own birding routine, this individual will just merge with yours! The avian experience for this individual isn't a dogged pursuit of any particular bird; in contrast, there is always room for welcome distractions—plant, animal, or mineral!

Consider the egret: At one with the marsh reeds, feeling the wind gently ruffle its wings.

The following light-hearted quiz is for curious readers who may want to get a jump on narrowing down their "possible" Type. Have fun!

Choose only the phrases that are absolutely your feathers! **Count the number of rows you checked that are of the same color; enter those numbers on the last row.**	
	I am known for my tough feathers and talons.
	I am disappointed when friends don't express appreciation about what I have done for them.
	My binoculars are focused on a direction that will result in success.
	Birding is meant to be a joyful, happy experience, not sitting around to see a particular bird.
	My metaphorical binoculars are focused on gaining more and more information.
	Before I take action I am prepared and cautious.
	I am a deeply passionate person and seek birding experiences that are awe-inspiring.
	My binoculars are focused on what needs improvement.
	Conflict—ugh! I prefer to choose the flight path of least resistance
	I spend a lot of time reading about various birds and migration patterns.

	I overdo and help others adjust their lenses even when my help is unsolicited.
	A good debate serves to energize me!
	When I look through the binoculars of others, it seems they always see better birds than me.
	I tend to focus what I can do better in all of my endeavors.
	I often second-guess or re-think my decisions.
	I'd much rather anticipate something than finish it.
	Birding is a hobby where I want to succeed—but not to distract me from my many goals.
	I waiver when given many choices.
	I reflect upon how I could improve my birding (and all) skills.
	Being prepared is my bottom line.
	My running script is, "What is my next accomplishment?"
	I can spend hours empathizing with a friend who is hurting.
	Don't beat around the bush—I prefer direct communication.
	I'm exhausted. I can't keep up with the needs of my flock.
	I imagine the best possible experiences and ultimate joy!

	I do *not* appreciate criticism. I am already hard enough on myself.
	When I fly, I gravitate to those who need my support.
	I have a sense of the dramatic, whether in life or when birdwatching.
	I am an efficient person.
	I often think of what can go wrong when planning an outing.
	I prefer to spend much of my time alone.
	I get bored with routine.
	I make fast, gut-based decisions.
	I will work hard and may sacrifice my own agenda to support my team.
	I focus on modeling what I perceive to be, the "right" way to behave.
	My binoculars are focused on others and how they perceive me.
	I have lots of stuff going on including bird-watching.
	People take their birding and life way too seriously.
	I share my bird knowledge sparingly, mainly with those for whom I have respect.
	My binoculars are focused on any danger that lies ahead.

	I am my moods, and can experience ecstasy and sadness when birdwatching.
	I don't have much respect for people or birds that don't stand up for themselves.
	When I feel pressured, my feathers may get ruffled.

*Total #									
Type	1	2	3	4	5	6	7	8	9

*The higher the number the more likely you associate with that particular type.

Count the number of rows you checked that *are of the same color*; enter those numbers here and on the last row of the KEY ASSESSMENT, page 130.

PART II
ENNEAGRAM 1-9 BIRDER TYPES

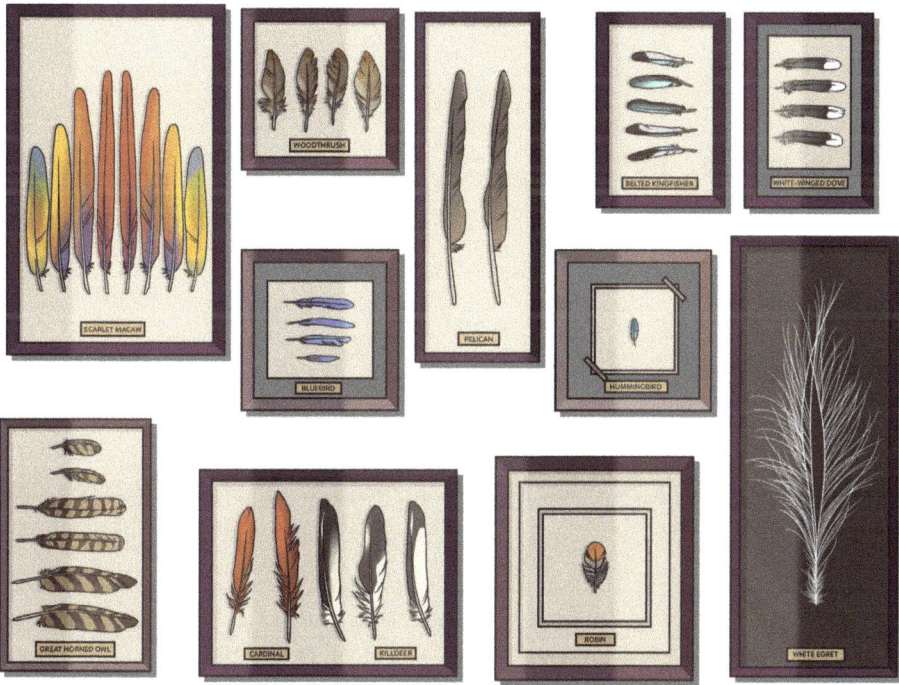

Note: Because the Enneagram Triads typically begin with the 2-3-4 Triad, the Types in Part II will proceed in this order:

The (Heart) Triad: Lovebirds
- Type 2
- Type 3
- Type 4

The (Brain) Triad: Bird Brains
- Type 5
- Type 6
- Type 7

The (Gut) Triad: Big Birds
- Type 8
- Type 9
- Type 1

*Authenticity is the daily practice of letting go of who we think
we are supposed to be and embracing who we are.*
Brené Brown, *The Gifts of Imperfection*

A Note on Awe

In a June 26, 2023, column in the *Washington Post*, cognitive scientist
and musician Maya Shankar shared excerpts from the commencement
address she delivered in May 2023, at the Juilliard School in New York.
Her reflections speak to how identities are formed and the importance
of making time for discernment to uncover our deepest motivations; to
discover what connects us to a broader whole. Below is an excerpt from
her address:

> We can learn to anchor our identities not to what we do—but
> to why we do it.

> Whether watching a beautiful sunset, or marveling at a new
> scientific discovery, feeling awe can help us tap into better ver-
> sions of who we are as people. We feel more connected to the
> broader whole, to something bigger than ourselves.

> And so, as you begin to anticipate the joys and challenges that
> lie ahead, I hope these three lessons will inspire you: Look for
> opportunities to practice imaginative courage; remember that

why you do something is more important than what you do; and, whenever possible, try and seek out awe.

I found her reflections particularly powerful, especially as they relate to the core of the Enneagram's message for those of the heart triad:

> *. . . remember that why you do something is more important than what you do and, whenever possible, try and seek out awe.*

In the same way most of us slam on the brakes when we spot a turtle crossing in front of our car, we must one and all come to a full stop for moments of *awe*. While individuals in this triad may stop all of the endless *doing* to notice extraordinary moments of awe—a shooting star, the Northern Lights, a breaching whale—the path to grace is to find the extra in ordinary awe. To come to understand the sentiment expressed in Maya's quote, a deep knowing that every moment, whether a tiny feather floating from a nest, the silent flight of an egret at sunset, or a drop of dew on a spring crocus, is worthy of reverence.

TYPE 2
THE SUPPORTIVE BIRDER

The bluebird carries the sky on his back.
Henry David Thoreau

CARING. SEDUCTIVE. HELPFUL. The Type 2 perceives she must carry "the world" on her shoulders, and the sky is so very heavy—which makes this Thoreau quote so apropos for the Type 2. Maybe I'm projecting or, as a physical therapist, I am particularly tuned into posture, but I've noticed that bluebirds slouch. They really do. Check out a bluebird perched on a wire (side angle), and you will most definitely see a slump. The bluebird is carrying the sky on its back, and the Type 2s are carrying the needs of the world (translation: their friend network) on theirs. They don't realize this weighty burden is affecting their ability to stand up for themselves or to balance their own needs with the needs of others.

The passion of the Type 2 is *pride*, and this is one of the more difficult of the passions to grasp, or for people in general to understand. For the Enneagram Type 2, pride is the need to be important to others, and hence they have an unconscious need to puff up their feathers. Underlying their willing and giving appearance, the Type 2 believes that everyone needs her and loves her and will pledge her undying return affection and support. Type 2s are seductive birds, and they will dance, coo, and woo you to get what they want.

Adaptive, strategic, the Type 2 bird and human will worm their way into your heart. When a 2 is *not* appreciated or loved, a form of shame kicks in, their passion of pride awakens them in the dead of night with the message, there *must be* something more I can say or do to *win over* the support of xyz; or if the midnight message is really harsh, it suggests something is wrong with *ME*.

The Type 2 pride gets truly *sticky* here, as Type 2s liken themselves to super glue, when in truth, their personal bond with others is closer to that of Velcro; they just don't know it. This realization—that their inter-personal attachments are not immutable—is when their relational bonds will become more authentic.

My own 2 pride became clear to me on a frigid winter morning, while reading on the front porch. I heard the smack of a bird hitting the window and peered out to find a rather dazed and disheveled hairy woodpecker (name, not hirsute) on the deck. I yelled out to my husband that we had a "woodpecker down" and he distractedly responded, "Hope he's okay." (He was watching a rather intense football game, to be fair.) Not to worry! I was already in motion, dishtowel in hand, to scoop up my wounded feathered friend and nurse him to a complete recovery. Ain't that just like a Type 2? Hairy's very own Florence Nightingale, running to help—armed with perhaps *unnecessary* tools to provide *unsolicited* aid?

If you happen to know any Type 2s, ask them how many of these save-the-day moments they recall over the years. If I didn't have a stal-wart Type 8 in my life to point out the, heretofore, uncalled for nature of my actions, many an unconscious rescue would proceed. My inner voice (of pride) whispers, "Well done, you!" Thus the reflection in the Type 2 savior-bird metaphorical window—we don't take the time to see through it; instead we see our own glowing reflection and act on impulse. And so as not to leave you hanging (or more apt, falling), by the time I swooped onto the deck "Harry" had flown, needing no help from me a'tall.

TYPE 2 FLOCK CHARACTERISTICS

- My binoculars are focused on others and how they perceive me.
- When I fly, I gravitate to those who need my support.

- When I meet others, I try hard to win them over.
- I think about becoming a master birder or taking a class to meet other bird lovers.
- I overdo and help others adjust their lenses even when my help is not requested.
- I am disappointed when friends don't express appreciation about what I have done for them.
- I'm exhausted. I can't keep up with the needs of my flock.
- I enjoy advising others and almost everyone wants my advice.
- I befriend almost everyone.

If these statements resonate, you might identify as a Type 2.

TYPE 2, SELF-PRESERVATION SUBTYPE/COUNTERTYPE (SP-2): GUARDED

I heard a bird so sing, whose music,
to my thinking, pleased the king.
William Shakespeare

The SP-2 Countertype is of a different nature than the typically perceived action-oriented 2 you know and appreciate. This true-blue bird is just so damn adorable, charming all comers with a stunning flash of color—while their human counterpart charms with humor and whimsy. The seduction for the SP-2 is a childlike, youthful way of enchanting others to love them. Denying their dependency on others, this Type 2 is more anxious and less trusting—simultaneously desiring and fearing the loving relationships they so want and need. The issue for this person is that while she may want to stay in her perpetual nest, she will inevitably outgrow it; or worse, be pushed

out by circumstances beyond her control. In this regard, ambivalence can mean a hard fall for the bird or unrequited emotional intimacy for the birder. At some point, our feathered friend will find it necessary to decide: stay in this increasingly crowded, well-worn space or embrace her ability to fledge.

I'm willing to bet that if asked the question, "name an adorable bird" the eastern bluebird would top most folks' lists; in part because it is a bird known to the average non-birder. Personally, the bluebird's "adorable" reputation came to light during a lazy, summer-day conversation with my mother-in-law, Harriet. We were sharing a rocking-chair chat on the deck when we spotted a flash of blue! Harriet vehemently declared, "AARGH. A bluebird. Horrid bird. Nasty bird!" Well, I don't know about you, but my childhood memories of bluebirds in (just about) every Disney film portray the bluebird as a close-to-angelic bird presence on earth. Sweet, little birds tweeting love and joy. My inside-voice was thinking, "What the hell is she on about? Blasphemy!" But she continued her rant, "Thieving birds! Nest robbers!" Needless to say, my radar was up now; full-on bluebird defense mode. I was considering the notion of an avian criminal underworld when I realized that she had confused bluebird and blue jay! And while I hate to take sides, I was so relieved that the reputation of my coy, charming, little bluebird would remain unscathed! On a side-note, I recognized that I needed to pay attention to the notion of bird-biases, and that Harriet had a tendency to use malapropisms. Good to know.

Migration Flyway: From Dependent to Free

Me, me, me! While it may seem contradictory to the *"Don't worry, I've got you"* Type 2 reputation; SP-2 feels they are so adorable and loveable (think puppies and bunnies), that everyone will take care of them just because they exist! Whoa! What. A. Concept. Perhaps the cuteness-for-care gig sounds good to some, but this dependence comes with a strong dose of anxiety and ambivalence surrounding relationships. The harsh truth is that the SP-2 needs to become mindful of their reliance on others, trust their nest-mates, and take-a-flight. Consciously owning their dependency needs is the small price the SP-2 will pay for being on the wing and rising to their true potential.

TYPE 2, SOCIAL SUBTYPE (SOCIAL-2): AMBITIOUS

> *We may not know whether our understanding is*
> *correct or whether our sentiments are noble, but the*
> *air of the day surrounds us like spring, which spreads*
> *over the land without our aid or notice.*
> Abraham Joshua Heschel

While the SP-2 is all about adorable *cooing*, the Social-2 is about calculated *wooing* to achieve a position of power. Consequently, I selected the crow as the exemplar for the Social-2. Crows have a strategically generous nature and give each other (and sometimes humans and other species) gifts to establish bonds. Don't let your imagination go all "Oprah" here—we aren't talking a Porsche, more like a lovely, variegated leaf, or an acorn. In the Social-2 world, this gift may be information, status, technical support, and if necessary, "stuff." It isn't necessarily the size of the gift but its import, an act of deliberate giving that makes the Social-2 and the crow of like mind. Obviously, I can't speak to the crow's motivation, but I can speak to the motivation of the Social Type 2. The reciprocal bond and resultant esteem is the relational hook for the Social-2. In contrast to an act of unconditional giving, the Social-2 "gives to get"; basically, in the hope that she will gain group status and be gazed upon with admiration. In short, the Social-2 seeks power and influence and, consciously or unconsciously, is hoping for a trove of "good will" down the line.

An abundance of stories testify to the crows' reciprocity in the form of gift giving. According to biologists John Marzluff and Tony Angell in their book, *Gifts of the Crow*, crows not only understand the benefit of reciprocating past acts that benefited them, they also anticipate the future reward—like Social-2s. Furthermore, hear this: they will balk at doing work for less reward than a peer is receiving! Ouch. Do I hear a bit of corvid manipulation in this reciprocal dance? You betcha. In fact, crows and 2s display impressive self-control, and will wait for a better reward, be it a chunky seed treat or a promotion. This behavior requires the capacity to assess the relative reward gain in relation to the cost of waiting; not to mention the reliability of the purveyor of said reward. Bottom line, do not underestimate the intuitive capabilities of crows and Social-2s to create bonds that will help them lead the flock and earn recognition. Bloody hell! Might crows resort to *Murder*?!

Migration Flyway: From Ambitious to Authentic

A beneficial undertaking for Social-2s is to close their social-compensation account. Cash out of the ego-driven, strategic social-giving plan and reinvest in their own repressed feelings and needs. The crow is a symbol of change, and the Social-2 can change direction by aborting strategic giving and adopting an authentic approach. That's when she will reap the highest dividends.

The frame of mind that flying harder will take one higher is perhaps true, but non-reliance on the flock may result in a lonely journey. This individual will benefit by exploring her need for status and power versus authentic, meaningful feelings—underscoring the value of vulnerability in establishing deeper relationships. Understanding the concept of *authentic* relational reciprocity is the true feather in the cap for the Social-2. Their motto needs to shift from "give to get" to "to give is to receive." Implementing this approach will ultimately reap the Social-2's interpersonal capital, and if fortunate, a pile of acorns and gum wrappers.

TYPE 2, ONE-TO-ONE SUBTYPE: SEXUAL

Nature bonds, but it does not cling. If I were
to cling to the red bird, I'd have to cage him.
Richard Rohr

Wild-at-heart. Generous. Focused. The Type 2, One-to-One is known as a classic temptress, hoping the object of her affection will meet her needs. I suspect the average bear (#Yogi) may not view birds as seductive creatures, but I beg to differ; and this does not necessarily mean that *I* am smarter than the average bear; it merely means that I have witnessed more than a few seductive birds in my time. Most recently and quite notably: the dance of the red-capped manakin, aka, the moon-walking bird. There are over fifty species of manakins, sparrow-sized birds that live to perform elaborate courtship displays to impress females. The male manakin not only moonwalks on a twig of a branch, but also clicks and buzzes *while dancing;* a wing-vibration trick. I dare you to try it, but don't be callin' me from the ER. I can attest that this courtship display, which can go on for hours if there is a particularly sexy female nearby, is downright sensual. I was a complete goner from the first click and step, humming MJ's "Billie Jean" in my head. I so wish I could ask Michael if he created his moves after a trip to Costa Rica, but I digress.

Like our red-capped gigolo, this One-to-One Subtype is a seducer of that one desired person from whom he hopes to gain devotion in return. While twig-balancing seems like an ass-backward (literally) way to do it—the One-to-One Two Subtype gains the allegiance of an-other who will do just about anything for him. Why, you ask? So our One-to-One metaphorical dancing fanatic doesn't need to *have or express his own needs.* He is just manakin-irresistible, dancing his way into your heart so you will be a devoted fan. Unabashedly alluring, this 2 Subtype will be aggressive in his pursuit of that special someone, confident that at the end of the day, or dance, this person will meet his needs.

Migration Flyway: Irresistible to Independent

This bird needs serious boundaries. First, show a little pride and knock off the bird-vamp routine! Second, embrace your own feathers and stop molting just to lure others. In bird-terms, if you are a bluebird, find your own berries; stop trying to seduce some unsuspecting wren to door-dash your meals.

TYPE 2 NAVIGATION TIPS

- You can draft for a while, it's okay.
- While love takes flight, possessiveness clips wings.
- Practice random acts of anonymous giving and service.
- When you feel the urge to help or rescue, reflect on whether it is for your interest alone.
- Trim back—on *everything*!
- Preen your own feathers first.
- Question yourself when you are trying too hard to win the approval of another.
- Don't just say yes; try, "I'll think about it and get back to you." No is also highly recommended.

TYPE 3
THE ACCOMPLISHED BIRDER

*The daily hummingbird
assaults existence with improbability.*
Ursula K. Le Guin

SUCCESSFUL. ACCOMPLISHED. EFFICIENT. The hummingbird's message for humans, and particularly for the Type 3, is that you are beautiful for the unique hum and hue of *you,* not what you *do.* Through the Enneagram, might all humans be able to see one another *in a different light,* especially during times of misunderstood intentions? Could we learn to recognize the "unique hue" of one another and thus, better relate in times of inexplicable joy or devastating grief?

Apparently, scientists have known for several decades that birds can see many colors that humans can't. Our retina's three cones, red, blue, and green, limit the range of hues we can detect. But most birds have another cone type that detects ultraviolet light—thus opening up an added dimension of combinations—unique shades of ultraviolet. Given this ocular super-power, perhaps birds can actually see other birds in a completely different light. At the conclusion of a study by Richard Prum and colleagues, they established that hummingbirds' super-saturated plumage out-hued all other previously analyzed bird species. He concluded that the reason for this vibrancy goes beyond the practical theories (attracting mates, etc.). Rather, he surmised, "Birds are beautiful because they are beautiful

to themselves." Let that be our mantra as we explore the Subtypes of the Type 3.

TYPE THREE FLOCK CHARACTERISTICS

- My binoculars are focused on a direction that will result in success.
- When I fly, I fly high!
- I take courses so I can enhance my bird identification skills.
- Expanding my bird sightings is my goal.
- Birding is a hobby where I want to excel—but not take so seriously that it keeps me from my other goals.
- I have lots of stuff going on, including bird-watching.
- I am an efficient person, if nothing else.
- My bird sightings may not be all that rare or unique, but I have a long list.
- I tend to compete with other birders.
- I am not into relaxing, so I'm not likely to linger too long waiting for one bird.
- My running script is, "What is my next accomplishment?"

If these resonate, you might identify as a Type 3 birder.

TYPE 3, SELF-PRESERVATION SUBTYPE/ COUNTERTYPE (SP-3): AUTONOMOUS

If birds can glide for long periods of time, then why can't I?
Orville Wright

The SP-3 has no need for admiration or accolades; instead their desire is to do *good*, to create an example "for good." Definitely not the stereotypical profile of the other Type 3s. Rather than image, the SP-3 is focused on ethics and doing the *right thing* as judged by social consensus. While this odd duck presents as cool and put together, he may be paddling like hell underneath the water, fearful and worried about security. But turbulence aside, this Subtype is a resourceful Type 3 and ultimately provides an example to all of us: that working hard truly does "pay off."

About ten years ago, in the aftermath of Hurricane Katrina, I read and immediately saved a *New York Times* opinion editorial on resilience: "What the Sparrows Told Me" by Trish O'Kane (August 16, 2014). The piece spoke of grief and despair surrounding the aftermath of the devastating storm. The piece recounted one woman's journey to heal by watching the "sparrow show."

> Each morning I sat on that back stoop and watched those sparrows. Instead of wondering what was going to happen to the city, to the Gulf Coast, to the planet, I started wondering why one sparrow was hogging all the seed. I started thinking about their resilience, their pluck, their focus on immediate needs. If they couldn't find food, they went somewhere else. If they lost a nest, they built another. They had no time or energy for grief. They clung to the fence in raggedy lines, heckling one another like drunken revelers on Bourbon Street.

The talented writer of this piece told her students that birds are a gift to help us get through each day, a way to enjoy the world while we change it, so that young people, everywhere, have a chance. Her prophetic words are even more resonant as I write this book in 2023, with the true effects of climate change wreaking havoc across the globe. With insight, Trish advised her students that when world events feel inexplicably horrible *to walk outside, listen for a minute, find a cardinal, woodpecker, or the ever-industrious sparrow—and see what they're up to.* Her belief, and I concur with my whole being, is that this small action, a five-minute pause, will likely not save the planet, but that it might save *us*, one bird at a time.

Thinking back, at the time I read her piece, I thought naively that a disaster of that magnitude could not be matched. In a matter of days, Hurricane Katrina had left a trail of death and destruction, and the narrative of countless lives changed. And here I am in January of 2023 admitting the depth of my naiveté. In the subsequent years after that storm, our planet has experienced both natural and human-created devastation of proportional magnitude, including tsunamis, wild fires, earthquakes, and volcano eruptions. Some of us can still summon the feelings of abject fear and grief that came in the wake of 9/11. And we are re-experiencing these same emotions in the aftermath of a three-year global pandemic that has spawned incredible social isolation and loneliness that, I dare say, none of us would have imagined. In hindsight, I have to question in what Shangri-La I existed.

So, I am calling on all sparrows to heal us. Why sparrows? Sparrows represent the industrious and never-flagging resilience that the Type 3 embodies and the planet needs so desperately. The SP-3 strives for virtue, and virtue is what the author experienced as she witnessed the sparrows' re-building in the face of adversity and sorrow. I have faith that, as an Enneagram-community, we have the power to envision a healed planet.

The author and philosopher, Iris Murdoch, is one of many authors who write of the power of nature to shift consciousness:

> Beauty is the convenient and traditional name of something which art and nature share, and which gives a fairly clear sense to the idea of quality of experience and change of consciousness. I am looking out of my window in an anxious and resentful state of mind, oblivious of my surroundings, brooding perhaps on some damage done to my prestige. Then suddenly I observe a hovering kestrel. In a moment, everything is altered. The brooding self with its hurt vanity has disappeared. There is nothing now but kestrel. And when I return to thinking of the other matter, it seems less important. And of course this is something which we may also do deliberately: give attention to nature in order to clear our minds of selfish care.

It is my sincere belief and hope that the gifts of the SP-3, in concert with the sparrows and kestrels, will focus our collective lens on the circle of life, on resilience, on hope.

Migration Flyway: From Autonomy to Inter-Dependence

You don't always have to be doing something.
You can just be, and that's plenty.
Alice Walker

This Type 3 can truly gain new height by drafting a
while, connecting and relying on others rather than
going it alone. If she migrates to Type 9, she may learn
to merge rather than going solo—or at least allow herself
to slow down and stop working so very hard, to get
in touch with and express her true feelings. If
she is brave, she will make space for her emotions and needs, using them to ride the winds
of change.

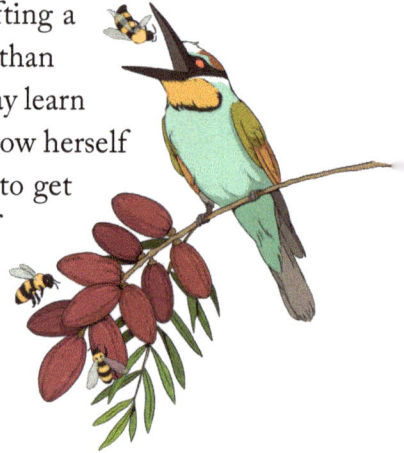

TYPE 3, SOCIAL SUBTYPE (SOCIAL-3): PRESTIGE

The world presents itself in two ways to me. The world as a
thing I own, the world as a mystery I face. What I own is a
trifle, what I face is sublime. I am careful not to waste what I
own; I must learn not to miss what I face.
Abraham Joshua Heschel

The Social-3 has an outstanding way with words and can frame comments carefully to maximize the impact on her audience. Socially brilliant
and keen to bask in the spotlight, this is the individual that many view as
the archetype of the Type 3—socially adept and quick to create alliances
with those who will enhance her life and birding success. This is the 3 that
was literally born to hum, engine ready to rev, while the rest of us are content to idle a while. Competitive by nature, this is the Type 3 that will be
eager to let you know that not only is she a birder, she is a *successful* birder.

However, Social-3s are prone to fall into the trap of, in the immortal words of T. S. Eliot: *We had the experience but missed the meaning.* I would like to thank Eliot for his wisdom, particularly as it applies to this particular Subtype. For the Social-3, it is important to recognize the difference between the façade of their own image (or images that reflect their own visage) and their *real* image, especially as it relates to the experience of authentic feelings. Prestige is the focus on the Social-3, which translates to an influential and achievement-oriented individual. On the birding *Big Count* days—you can bet your last tail feather that the Social-3 birder will be up at dawn and ready to compete! Their goal being successful sightings and spotting the most birds by any means possible.

A number of years ago we went on a birding trip with a guide that had advertised on his website photos of birds that we would likely see over the course of our day-long excursion. What we failed to realize is that the vast majority of the birds we would see would be through the viewfinder of our guide's camera; the *post snap* photo after the bird flew away. Our guide, I fear, was an uninspired Social-3 who definitely was not soaring. He had moved from sharing the actual bird-moment with us to being wed to his bird images.

This *misguided* fellow would literally pounce in front of us, situate his tripod, and start clicking, despite our protestations (*where IS the bird!*) and frustrations *(is it still THERE?)*. And after snapping the bird's "head shots" he would then say, "Wow! Did you *see* it?" Our guide was all show, and not in touch with the essence of being in nature with the birds. My advice for this guide and others of this Subtype is to read the end of the aforementioned quote by T. S. Eliot: *and approach to the meaning restores the experience in a different form.* This deep work for the Social-3 surrounds disentangling their perception that their image is more loveable than their real self, which in contrast to their belief, can diminish their value.

Migration Flyway: From Prestige to Authenticity

There is an ancient Greek proverb dating to 1539 that states, "One swallow doesn't make a summer,"—a warning to not assume that one accolade or pretty image equals success or gains one a lifetime achievement award. Instead, each achievement is but one step toward building a strong life resume. Far be it from me to upend Greek wisdom, not to mention their myriad architectural achievements. Using a flight analogy, I don't know about you, but I'd much prefer to fly aboard a sturdy plane than a gorgeous one that has mechanical issues. In other words, when I'm at thirty-thousand feet, I couldn't care less if I'm on a pretty plane—give me a solid engine. Migration for Social-3s proceeds more efficiently and safely by recognizing that image is not only *not everything*, but that their life-ride will be so much smoother by realizing that it is their vulnerability, including setbacks and failures, that will profoundly broaden their horizons.

TYPE 3, ONE-TO-ONE SUBTYPE: SUPPORTIVE

I once asked a bird, "How is it that you fly in this gravity of darkness?" She responded, "Love lifts me."
Hafez

Have you ever been beguiled, mesmerized, or inveigled by another? If so, you may well have been under the spell of a Type 3, One-to-One. Sweet, shy, and uninterested in prestige, this 3 Subtype is all about *you*; well, sort of. You see, they win by wooing you, and in making you glow, they shine. More emotional than the other Type 3 Subtypes, these 3s peel off the mask and rely on their beauty and appeal to be enough to achieve your unerring adoration. The concept of *being good* for this Subtype is different from that of the SP-3; it is exhibited more in terms of sexual or personal appeal than morality. This person will be more likely to avoid the pretense and will *express* rather than *cover* his feelings. While the Social-3 is flying high, the understated Type 3, One-to-One is content to be the wind beneath another's wings. This 3 Subtype can be mistaken as a Type 2 or Type 7 due to their positive and genuine support for others' achievements.

I vividly recall the day I experienced this type of avian sexual appeal watching a male hummingbird's courtship dance, as though he only had wings to dance for her. We encountered him, suspended in mid-air, just off our hiking path in a tiny cove of soft, green leaves. It was as if he were a twirling puppet being maneuvered on an invisible, spider-web string. An ardent tiny-dancer. We were transfixed, mesmerized, and unable to turn away our gaze, while at the same time ashamed to be peering at what felt like such an intimate moment. He was at once coy and intense, with no apparent awareness of our presence; he had but one sole purpose: to flutter his quickly-beating-heart out for the female perched on the branch above. This tiny-dancer, in the wild jungle of Corcovado National Park, exhibited qualities reminiscent of this One-to-One Subtype; his sole interest being one of sex-appeal and dazzling beauty.

Migration Flyway: From Supportive to Autonomous

The One-to-One Type 3 will benefit from becoming more conscious of his own flight pattern rather than continually elevating that of others; making room for his own desires and needs. While helping others comes naturally, he will find that by sharing personal challenges, others will relate to him on a more authentic plane. After all, to be human is to acknowledge one's interdependence.

TYPE 3 NAVIGATION TIPS

- Stop flying. Take a rest in your nest.
- Don't plan: find hammock, put down phone, close eyes.
- Find a friend to walk beside your authentic self.
- Stop, listen, and feel lest you miss the soliloquy of the wood thrush and the white-throated sparrow.
- Allow yourself to be appreciated simply for your feathers, not how high you can fly.
- Admit your perceived disasters to at least one person.
- A practice of daily meditation is not for the birds, it is for *you*.
- Notice, stop and appreciate the birds and the bees.

Our measurements of social success, fabricated hierarchies, attractiveness, money, are benign, useless. When we bird, we are not ruled by our possessions, by looks, by likes. We mean no harm, have nothing to hide. To be among the birds is to have an experience that cannot be bought, cannot be imitated. It asks nothing but holds all we need to be truly awake.

Adapted from Mira Ptacin

TYPE 4
THE EMPATHIC BIRDER

We cannot be more sensitive to pleasure
without being more sensitive to pain.
Alan Watts

COMPLEX. FEELING. UNIQUE. For Type 4s, their sensitivity is a double-edged sword. The message of the Type 4 for the rest of us is to remember that the capacity to feel deeply will make the good times that much sweeter. Watts's quote truly captures the experience of many 4s: being fully alive means accepting both the agony and ecstasy in equal measure. This requires one to be at peace with pleasure and with pain, with clear blue skies and torrential rain. To understand that to tamp down difficult emotions, as if extinguishing their flame, might alleviate suffering yet will prevent fully experiencing the intensity of joy. While this level of emotional intensity feels like burdensome plumage to many, the Type 4 basks in the warmth of emotive feathers.

When picturing an avian Type 4, the statuesque silhouette of the great blue heron comes to mind, like a palace guard, a feathered sentry at the threshold of marshlands. For twenty-eight seasons' passing we have watched our *own* great blue from the comfort of soul-nourishing windows at our Folly Beach home, aptly named, *Heron's Wait*. And while our bodies have weakened and succumbed to the tides of time, her progeny continue to stand strong at the edge of the water. She waits. Shrouded in dark blue robes, the gentle whitecaps swathing her feet, a widow's watch at the edge of a shimmering sea. To observe the great blue heron is to feel the intricate, exquisite suffering of all of the Type Fours; their thirst never quite quenched.

> *May she fly to peaceful waters*
> *With her regal sons and daughters*
> *May my eyes shine with her dreams*
> *The world is more than it seems.*
> Deborah Levoy, *Blue Heron*

TYPE FOUR FLOCK CHARACTERISTICS

- My binoculars are focused on finding deep meaning and a unique view.
- When I fly, I experience great highs and lows.
- I have a sense of the dramatic, whether in life or when birdwatching.
- When I look through the binoculars of others, it seems they always see better birds.
- I am a deeply passionate person and seek birding experiences that are awe-inspiring.
- Deep down I don't think I'll ever be a *real* birder.
- I am my moods and can experience ecstasy and defeat when birdwatching.
- I've been told I have a great eye for beauty, and that shows in many of my pursuits.
- When I feel good about myself, I feel good about my coalescence with nature.

- I can spend hours empathizing with a friend who is hurting.

If these resonate, you might identify as a 4 birder.

TYPE 4, SELF-PRESERVATION SUBTYPE/COUNTERTYPE (SP-4): RESOLUTE

Our eyes are so often drawn to grand majesties—a vivid sunset or an expansive landscape—but the smallest of things has value, a story of its own, and a place in the world.
Claudia Retter

Known as "reckless/dauntless," the Type 4 Countertype, the SP-4, tends to suffer in silence and may behave similar to a Type 7 or 3 by engaging in continuous activity as a way to keep sad feelings at bay and energize herself. While reading this section, you may want to play Gloria Gaynor's, "I Will Survive" or Queen's, "The Show Must Go On." *Inside the 4's heart is breaking, but the smile, still stays on,* because this individual has a desire, or more aptly stated, a *need* to be strong and endure; even going so far as to put themselves in challenging situations. The SP-4 faces obstacles and frustration by coming to terms with all of it, *it* being whatever is needed to survive. Don't be mistaken: this person experiences deep feelings but endures the discomfort, preferring the stoic route rather than the emotional flyway. This Type 4 can occasionally resemble a Type 1, translating her deep feelings into the pursuit of justice for those in need. And surprisingly, a subset of SP-4s can display a lightness of being not shared by the other Subtypes—a downright chipper *joie de vivre*. I know, call me crazy—a Type 4 with a spring in their step? It's a world gone mad!

I vividly recall meeting what I believed to be a Self-preservation Type 4 on the edge of a small, crystalline pool at a lodge in Costa Rica. It was dusk (the time of day when all true Type 4s appear). To my ears, some of the most gut-wrenching bird songs reverberated across the jungle at this time of day; the chestnut-mandibled toucan (Swainson's) and the great tinamou. If I close my eyes and recall their songs, I find myself back in time, immersed in a many-hued sea of green leaves, inhaling the scent of some sweet, unknown flower, and the faint sound of moving water to the steady dip, kick, and breath of a swimmer. The spell of it all, a moment of nirvana. And then I heard them, descending like a troop of spider monkeys, but not; instead, a throng of small children, shrieking, splashing, leaping into the pure pool of, what was, bliss. Now, noise and cacophony. Mayhem.

No bird soars too high if he soars with his own wings.
William Blake

I turned to witness a gentle swimmer, rising out of the water in the rutilant light, the rays of the sun behind the trees giving her the appearance of a jungle goddess. With a wry, weary countenance she uttered only one phrase before descending back into the rippling waters, "*Paradise Lost.*" One phrase, one moment in time, but the lifetime stoic lament of the SP-4; *we will endure this sorrow, with a weary resignation that nothing so enchanting will last forever.*

Migration Flyway: From Resolute to Lightness of Being

You perceive you must tenaciously persevere against the gale, even when the winds have subsided to a gentle breeze. Can you recognize the lightness of your own being, your own buoyant feathers? Release your locked perch and distance yourself from the burdens of the land. Swoop and dive beneath the billowing clouds and appreciate the freedom only soaring can bring.

TYPE 4, SOCIAL SUBTYPE (SOCIAL-4): SHAME

Empathy begins with understanding life from another person's perspective. Nobody has an objective experience of reality. It's all through our own individual prisms.
Sterling K. Brown

While Cyndi Lauper might sing for Type 7s, *girls just wanna have fun,* and the SP-4s are belting out Queen's beat, someone else has to sing the lament of the Social-4: *we just want to be understood!* I'm thinking, like, *any* song by Taylor Swift?

But if music's not your jam, there's a new book by the author Susan Cain titled *Bittersweet*. Susan is a self-professed Enneagram Type 4, and the subtitle of *Bittersweet* is the motto of many-a-Type 4: *How Sorrow and Longing Make Us Whole*. I'm thinking, yikes, that sounds like a load of laughs! However, this is the exact message Social-4s want the rest of us not only to get, but truly consider trying on. Social 4s have a deep (as in well-water deep) understanding of the power of sorrow to *complete us;* and Susan's goal in *Bittersweet* is to help the rest of us mortal types understand the transcendent space that Type 4s occupy on the planet.

But if neither reading nor music is your jam, know this: the Social-4 is a timid bird, unwilling to share her desires. And while humans and birds generally express their sexuality (some with seemingly ridiculous antics; note: I am not specifying which species), the Social-4 has a nestful of shame when relating to any true expression of lust or anger.

If you have ever had an otherworldly feeling in ordinary places, you may have had a "Social-4" experience of reality. I recall one such time about a year ago, when I awoke before dawn on a fall morning to a dense fog on the marsh and the quiet that only early-morning risers know—sheer, utter silence.

To be sure, this is not an experience I aspire to—I covet sleep. But this morning was different, and I rose to a luminous, full moon through high windows and lit candles, feeling a sense of longing and belonging all at once. In that moment, I channeled Social-4 energy—that bittersweet feeling. Sliding open the door onto the marsh, I inhaled the moist air and thought of a bird that does not migrate to warm, low-country waters—the common loon. This moment beckoned the bird call that had eluded me for sixty-five years—often described as a deep yodel or moan. A call that is symbolic of the Maine and Alaskan wildernesses and resonates with an ever-present longing for what is "out there" that we do not understand. I shivered and pulled my robe a bit tighter in my imaginings.

I conjecture that my "loon longing" is a routine feeling for the Social-4. From the first time I ventured to Maine, with its rock-rimmed coastal waters, I deigned it my "soul place" (I now know I'm in good company with many Type 4s), and I made it my quest to find my way back on numerous occasions. I saw salmon spawning, Caribou grazing, and I cycled the winding carriage trails of Acadia National Park; but not once did I hear the call of the *common* loon, as though the name itself is a bit of a cruel joke on me; *everyone* has heard a common loon. At least I don't have to evade the question anymore; it's now written here for all to know: I'm loon-less.

Migration Flyway: From Shelter to Freedom

> *Two hearts united*
> *will break down a mountain.*
> Persian proverb

The prevailing winds for those identifying with this 4 Subtype are a sense of shame, mingled with a desire to earn understanding for their suffering. Like a bird that has lost her feathers, the Social 4 is constantly seeking support, particularly from colleagues and groups with whom they associate. Perhaps birds, acting as winged messengers, can help her re-grow her metaphysical lost feathers and remind her that she can fly solo and when ready, venture away from the safety of her nest—despite the fierce emotional winds she might encounter.

TYPE 4, ONE-TO-ONE SUBTYPE: RIVALRY

> *How can I see so clearly that everything I love or care about*
> *is an illusion, and yet—for me, anyway—all that's worth*
> *living for lies in that charm?*
> Donna Tartt, *The Goldfinch*

Intensely competitive, the One-to-One Type 4 has a deeply-rooted drive to attain what he desires; often leaving niceties behind. Unlike the somewhat sad expression of the Social-4, this 4 is more mad, and mutes his frustration in envious anger. This Type 4 wants to win, adopting an arrogant attitude to cover his inferiority.

By way of example I recall my first trip to Costa Rica and my ardent desire to see the stunning quetzal, indigenous to the region of Monteverde. And, I *swear* to you, I *might have seen* a quetzal. I'm *pretty darn sure,* but that startling flash of incandescent blue feathers was just so quick! If you are a birder holding a black marker while reading this you'll be sadly (perhaps a bit smugly?) crossing quetzal off of my bird list. In British bird slang, I was *dipped* on sighting a quetzal; and that didn't sit well with me.

This elusive bird tale is analogous to the conundrum faced by One-to-One Type 4s, as they have a strong desire to obtain the object of their desire; and when unrealized they become demanding. They feel that the true gold is just *over the rainbow* and thus, singularly focused, they unfortunately often miss out on the array of colors they encounter along the way. Individuals of this Subtype, similar to all 4s, are seeking a way out of their mediocre life to discover the life they were intended to live; one with depth and intensity. Yet, due to their discontented nature, this One-to-One is often left holding a startling blue feather.

Migration Flyway: From Competition to Cooperation

The One-to-One Type 4 will benefit by burrowing under his own downy feather blanket; appreciating that when life feels harsh, he can find comfort in his own nest. This will serve as a reminder that the person who can fully experience the present moment is never hopeless. Hopelessness is an experience whereby a person can only achieve joy winging in one direction. When we can imagine only one way to be happy, we don't recognize the fullness and possibilities of the moment. We are grounded if our one way to be on the wing is taken away from us. As the diaphragm moves without thought to bring breath to life, expand your chest, expose your tender heart, and spread your wings—appreciating the slow rhythmic motion of being.

Moon tonight,
Beloved —
When twilight
Has gathered together
The ends
Of her soft robe
And the last bird-call
Has died.

Moon tonight—
Cool as a forgotten dream,
Dearer than lost twilights
Among trees where birds sing
No more.

Gwendolyn Bennett

TYPE 4 NAVIGATION TIPS

- Remember, ordinary can be beautiful too.
- Keep it simple but significant.
- Don't make your life a crisis center.
- Listen to other birders' successes—without feather envy.
- Keep an eye out for emoting too much with birds—they will survive the winter storms. Really.
- Don't give up on your "natural" gifts—remind yourself that you, too, can soar.
- Focus on the bird in the hand, rather than constantly pining for the birds in the bush.
- Nurture an unconditional relationship with nature—and apply that to friendships.

Joy fell from the sky.
Let us not tell our children a story that begins,
Once in the forests there was a Laughingthrush
We had met with Chestnut-eared Laughingthrush
Again and again, there in the heart of the heart
Of the forest, there where our fellow humans
Had not cleared, hunted, trapped, and defoliated Life out of
existence. There sweet thrush–like notes may stream yet as
water over rows of stones. Others there sang the songs of their
species too. And our bodies also lighter with laughter.
Hai-Dang Phan, "Canto of the Chestnut-eared Laughingthrush"

TYPES 5-6-7 (HEAD) TRIAD
BIRD BRAINS

Birds are born twice: once from the egg,
and again when they learn to fly.
Unattributed

A Note on Nesting

I admit to experiencing a
sense of elation in early spring
when I see my first flash of blue-
bird-blue color as the eastern bluebird swoops from
his nest in the birdhouse on
the top of the pole in the corner
of our donkey corral. While we have not banded this lil' fella, I feel a certain peace in believing he has returned from his worldly travels to migrate
to our North Carolina farm, he has returned "home." For humans, a nest
is a place of safety—where we feel most able to reveal our truest selves;
be that kind or snarky, easygoing or rigid. It is a place to be nurtured, and
provides us a safe space to grow our metaphorical *brave* feathers.

The word *nestle*, a verb from middle English, *nestlen*, or Old English,
nestlian, literally means "build a nest, make or live in a (bird's) nest." The
word *nestle* calls to mind my morning yoga practice and the value of our
closing Shavasana, when we quiet our busy minds and calm our breath-
ing; settling before rising to the demands of the day.

Those of the head triad, are inclined toward mental-disquiet: forcast-
ing, imagining, mentally preparing. Of all types, the 5-6-7s know well the
import of upending looping thought patterns and settling the mind to
nourish the body, mind, and spirit. What may be most vital for those of

this triad is the ability to seek to find a nest of mindful resilience before choosing the moment to take wing.

> *Strange to have come through the whole century and find*
> *that the most interesting thing is the birds. Or maybe it's*
> *just the human mind is more interesting when focusing on*
> *something other than itself.*
> John Hay

TYPE 5
THE OBSERVANT BIRDER

WISE. RECLUSIVE. CALM. If you aren't certain you know a Type 5, you may have to be patient, and akin to uncorking a fine wine, b-r-e-a-t-h-e, wait for them. Type Fives have much to teach all of us about the art of observing, the power of listening, and embracing stillness. Like a scene from a British mystery, the Type 5 will spy you long before you see him. Similar to owls, Type 5s invite us to move through life more quietly, to notice sights and sounds that may otherwise elude us. To an extroverted Type 2, like me, the owl sets a high branch for how I could aspire to navigate the world. I read somewhere that given the owl's unassuming presence and noiseless flight, they point out the value of not standing *out*, but fitting *in* to the world. Quite the exception to the general rule of the current social media notice-me culture. There's great wisdom to be had in exploring the art of camouflage, and much to learn from the unobtrusive owl and the discerning Type 5.

TYPE 5 FLOCK CHARACTERISTICS

- My binoculars are focused on locating more and more information.
- When I fly, I prefer to fly solo.
- I am a patient, observant birder.

- I spend a lot of time reading about various birds and migration patterns.
- I prefer to spend time birding alone.
- I enjoy stepping away from birdwatching to reflect and catalog what I have seen.
- I am interested in self-guided bird courses and independent learning.
- I think of a life as a naturally evolving mystery, of sorts, and I am immersed in all aspects.
- I share my bird knowledge sparingly, mainly with those for whom I have respect.
- I do not *guess* when identifying birds; I use discretion.

If these resonate, you might identify as a Type 5 birder.

TYPE 5, SELF-PRESERVATION SUBTYPE (SP-5): SANCTUARY

There was an article in the *New York Times* about a year ago that suggested that wild creatures, their very existence, reveal to us that some aspects of the universe are unknown to us. To some people, these wild unknowns are of no consequence as they busy themselves dealing with the many *knowns* on their full plates. Yet, to a Type 5, the search for deeper knowledge of the mysteries buried in a sea of wildness is an irresistible lure.

I had a visceral SP-5 experience while birding in a canyon forest just south of Tucson, Arizona. In the rapidly fading afternoon light I heard a deep, guttural hum of unknown origin and direction. If you are an alert and cautious person or anything like me ('fraidy cat), and hear a deep, dusky throated hum or harsh croaking sound in dense wood—your first instinct might be to *turn tail and run like hell!* I can't blame you for making this instinctual choice, especially if you've watched as many British mysteries as me. But I beseech you to go with your second instinct, which is to grab your binoculars and begin the slow and patient search for a brilliant metallic-green and red bird, the elegant trogon. Why is patience required? Because the trogon, much like the SP-5, can be a reclusive sort. If you are fortunate enough to stay in stillness and listen with rapt attention, he might show himself to you and impart a modicum of forest wisdom.

Trogons, like SP-5s have a desire for *sanctuary,* and the mid-canopy forest provides that desired physical protection. Sitting quietly perched, like the SP-5, the elegant trogon is a keenly observant bird; oft termed a "sit and wait" predator. The trogon, like the SP-5 would prefer to remain hidden, nestled in a cavity, as the exterior world and people are threatening. This 5 Subtype has a deep need to feel "safe"; expressing the needs and desires that come with being "human" are far too unpredictable and taxing. Instead, individuals of this Subtype learn to survive behind figurative and real walls. This wise 5, knowing the terrain, gives up his secrets slowly.

> How do the geese know
> when to fly to the sun?
> Who tells them the seasons?
> How do we, humans, know when
> it is time to move on?
> As with the migrant birds, so surely
> with us, there is a voice within,
> if only we would listen to it,
> that tells us so certainly when
> to go forth into the unknown.
>
> Elisabeth Kübler-Ross

Migration Flyway: From Sanctuary to Connection

I would suggest that all individuals are liberated when aligned with their human essence and that of their environs; but external connections can be particularly transformative for the Type 5. As though the universe is providing a summer break, or better, early retirement, from the endless quest for more and more protection before connection. Self-preservation 5s must retrieve the allegorical hammer to smash the castle walls and connect with the beckoning world—even when it inspires fear and discomfort—allowing in the light that will serve to illuminate their buried feelings and reveal a path to their heart.

TYPE 5, SOCIAL SUBTYPE (SOCIAL-5): IDEALISTIC

Sorrow, O sorrow, moves like a loose flock
of blackbirds sweeping over the metal roofs,
over the birches, and the miles.
One wave after another, then another, then the sudden
opening where the feathered swirl, illumined by dusk,
parts to reveal the weeping heart of all things.

Vievee Francis, "Clarity"

Social 5s are all about developing strong bonds with those individuals and groups with whom their ideals align. However, when forced or coerced to live out of alignment with their beliefs they will disengage rather quickly. They fly away into the still of the night. For the Social-5, the concept of *searching,* or more aptly, *longing,* is to find the ultimate meaning in life; a quest for the Holy Grail, for the extraordinary. *Ordinary* just won't do. This pursuit for Social-5s can present a bit of a conundrum in that they become disinterested in the rather humdrum facets of everyday life. The Social-5 can become so idealistic in his quest for the extraordinary, that he misses real connection with others and the beautiful-ordinary; simple wonders of life become uninspiring. This is regrettable, in that when relating to the knowledge and *attributes of people* the Social-5 might, at last, find the elusive extraordinary for which he is looking.

I've come to the conclusion that the blackbird is ubiquitous and elusive at the same time; a feathered-oxymoron. Think for a moment just how many song lyrics refer to the enigmatic, unattainable blackbird. Regretfully, I cannot quote the best of them due to the risk of one of the remaining Beatles suing me for copyright infringement (like that wouldn't be a lyrical-risk worth taking?! To be sued by a *Beatle).* But I need not write these famous blackbird lyrics, as you are most likely humming the tune in your mind. We all know of blackbirds singing in the "dark, black" night. Or perhaps you recollect a bit less-well-known lyric of catching ahold of blackbird wings that will carry us away on a sweet, spring day (do a Google search for these soulful, lovely tunes). So many songs allude to a sense of freeing ourselves from what binds us—of untethering our souls to find some mysterious, exceptional "other" that awaits us. This mirrors the Social-5 space, to transcend our fragile nature in search of the ultimate—whether ideals, characteristics, or sheer knowledge.

While there are many species of blackbird, my lens is focused on the red-winged blackbird whose characteristic call is well known to me, pealing over the ponds near our farm. Much like the Social-5, the male red-winged blackbird wears his heart and feelings on his "sleeve," in the hopes of attracting a mate, but also to ward away unwanted predators. If we pay close attention, the positions of his brilliant red epaulets—a streak of color, an angle of a shoulder, a thin line of yellow feathers—tell us a great deal about his motivation; to identify with the extraordinary. To spread his tiny wings and fly away from the fray.

Migration Flyway: From Idealistic to Ordinary

The Social-5s can benefit by flying out of the clouds down to earth to mingle with their emotional flock. To borrow from an idiom, this individual needs to recognize that all of his geese are *not* swans, and he not only needs, but will benefit from, a dose of humdrum. The Social-5's high ideals, while seemingly exceptional, are often unfounded and lacking in emotional weight. By mingling and sharing seeds of wisdom with the middling birds at the feeder, he has hope of finding actual, rather than idealized, relationships.

TYPE 5, ONE-TO-ONE SUBTYPE/ COUNTERTYPE): CONFIDENCE

Once you have understood the basic principle of being present as the watcher of what happens inside of you—and you understand it by experiencing it—you have at your disposal the most potent transformational tool.
Eckhart Tolle

The One-to-One Type 5 is a passionate person and seeks a partner that represents the ultimate mystical union—an experience of the divine in another human. These individuals seek partners who will be transparent and love them fully—flaws and all. As the Countertype of the Type 5, this 5 Subtype is intense, emotionally sensitive, and romantic. Often seen as iconoclasts, One-to-One 5s will avoid intimacy by *testing others* to determine if they meet their high standards and, sadly, this path often leads to disillusionment.

If you have studied the Enneagram, you are conjuring up an image of the Type 5; the person hanging out in the corner, dark shades, hoping to not be noticed. Or the one with the not-so-subtle lapel button that states, leave me the * alone! Au contraire, you may have mistakenly been judging all birds by their *covers*, or more specifically, their *covert* feather *colors*; and by now you know that is no way to judge a book, a person, or a bird.

May I introduce the macaw, a scarlet bird bedecked in feathered robes of crimson, green, and gold. At first pass the scarlet macaw's rainbow colors call to mind the riotous joy of the Type 7. When in flight, these birds resemble a carnival tent that has lost its bearing, swirling atop the jungle canopy. The macaws seem to be above it/us all—and certainly, of a different feather altogether.

I determined that this extraordinary, confident bird captured the qualities of the 5 Countertype. This striking member of the parrot family is not only loyal and wise, like all Type 5s—but akin to the One-to-One 5, he is a hopeless romantic, seeking his one and only dazzling, unrivaled life mate.

While the nectar of the One-to-One 5 is knowledge, the Costa Rican Osa Peninsula serves up beach almonds, definitely the *numero uno* food choice for the *lapa* (the Costa Rican name for scarlet macaw). The almond tree, when fruiting, is a definite "tell" if you want to find lapas. It seems they would be so obvious to spot, but you are much more likely to be pelted on the head by a discarded shell. If you can take the heat, join me in taking the long, blistering hike to find this beauteous pair of birds. I don't know about you, but I am a sucker for a steamy beach romance.

Migration Flyway: From Confidence to Clarity

Bird watching, whether huddled in a dense forest or sequestered on some remote mountain, is a quiet business; while engaging with people, in general, is a loud and messy business. *In working on themselves,* individuals of this Subtype can benefit from joining the hoi polloi and noticing the messiness of being human. By embracing the emotional up and down drafts that are a part of intimate relationships, the One-to-One Type 5 can stop testing others, and begin expressing true emotions.

TYPE 5 NAVIGATION TIPS

- You can benefit by shifting your binoculars to focus on feelings.
- Hang out at the feeder, break seed together.
- It's ok to trust another bird of a feather—flock together.
- Come down from your high perch. Get grounded.
- Go with your gut now and again.
- Stop studying, go with the flow.
- So-called common birds are beautiful, too.

> *I think the most important quality in a birdwatcher*
> *Is a willingness to stand quietly and see what comes.*
> *Our everyday lives obscure a truth about existence*
> *That at the heart of everything there lies a*
> *stillness and a light.*
> Lynn Thomson

TYPE 6
THE VIGILANT BIRDER

A bird is safe in its nest—
but that is not what its wings are made for.
Amit Ray

LOYAL. CAUTIOUS. PREPARED. The Type 6 is a bit of an enigma on the Enneagram spectrum. While all Type 6s deal with a sense of anxiety and their passion, fear, they approach these emotional responses with very different energies. Claudio Naranjo suggests that the Type 6 Subtypes are so distinct that it is a challenge to speak of just a singular Type 6; rather, he refers to three unique kinds of Type 6 that I will describe in this chapter.

As I've noted in previous Type descriptions, we often approach life as we approach birding, peering at the object of our attention through a very small binocular lens without seeing the whole of the surrounding landscape. Upon observing the behaviors of others, more often than not, we ascribe motivation and intent, extrapolating erroneous meaning based on our limited perspective. Sadly, this is the fallacy of the binocular view.

When this concept is applied to Type 6s, their lens tends to focus on the headwinds, or life's challenges. Type 6s anticipate the obstacles ahead and how they might navigate each situation to experience the least amount of damage. Type 6s would rightly argue that this is their particular skill set; preparing for impending: Peril. Danger. Threats. However, to quote Hamlet, "Ay, there's the rub"! In focusing almost exclusively on headwinds, Type 6s are not as aware or appreciative of tailwinds, the supportive and encouraging aspects of life. As all birds know (especially Irish birds), when the wind is at your back, the world gives ya' a wee break, a lift; we can fly more easily.

Enneagram teacher and scholar, Beatrice Chestnut, uses the term *different temperatures* to describe the three Type 6 Subtype approaches to facing fear: warmth, duty, and strength. And temperature is an apt metaphor to describe the preoccupation of many-a-six. I reckon that birds cackle at humans' absurd preoccupation with weather. We incessantly discuss the highs and lows, fret over appropriate clothing, broadcast the temperature and chances of rain/sleet/snow a minimum of three times a day and then continue to discuss it ad nauseam.

In stark contrast, birds: sing a chorus to the dawning of day during the cool morning air; lie low in midday heat; and serenade us as the sun descends toward the horizon. They keep it simple and sweet. Pema Chödrön's quote below resonates of self-compassion and our daily choice to lean into the rhythms of life's fluctuating course, rather than trying to control it. Her encouraging words speak to the heart of the Self-preservation Type 6s, to ground themselves when overwhelmed by life's inevitable ups and downs.

You are the sky.
Everything else is just weather.
Pema Chödrön

TYPE 6 FLOCK CHARACTERISTICS

- My binoculars are focused on any danger that lies ahead.
- When I fly, I am prepared and cautious.
- I often think of what can go wrong when planning an outing.
- I watch the weather and have concerns about droughts and flooding.
- I find myself questioning so-called experts.
- I tend to employ both wit and wisdom in life.
- I almost always second-guess my decisions.

- I am dutiful and try my best to do the "right thing."
- Being prepared is my bottom line.
- I like an order in most of my endeavors.
- When I hear *new and improved*, I tend to be skeptical.

If these phrases resonate, you might identify as a Type 6.

TYPE 6, SELF-PRESERVATION SUBTYPE (SP-6): HIGH ALERT AND INDECISIVE

That the birds of worry and care
fly above your head, this you cannot change.
But that they build their nests in your hair,
this you can prevent.

Chinese Proverb

Warm. Supportive. Indecisive. The SP-6 is the most phobic Type 6. Not trusting their own internal compass, they seek security through others; protection via alliances. Similarly, birds have an instinctual preparatory system—and the flock responds accordingly; it's called a "bird plow." In brief, birds sense when potential danger is approaching and move out ahead and away from it. Take note the next time you're walking on a forest trail when you observe the birds all flying out of a tree in one unified direction. No sci-fi or Hitchcock movie here; this *flock-flight* is a bird plow and signifies they've noted an approaching threat: owl, falcon, or you; they are flying toward a more secure location. So, be it a sparrow, starling, or SP-6, all are in tune with approaching perils, and if you are listening, they will let you know the responsible protocols.

With all of the soaring freedom that comes with being a bird also comes the reality that birds, like most SP-6s, must remain constantly vigilant and for some, on high alert. Inherent in the nature of the SP-6 is the tendency to doubt everybody and everything—at least until otherwise convinced. As one who has facilitated hundreds of Enneagram workshops, I tease that I can spot the Type 6s (and 5s) a mile away; as they are the ones eyeing me with overt suspicion! As a Type 2, endlessly aware of and seeking others' approval and appreciation, I unfortunately hone into their narrowed gaze and wrinkled brows. I need to remind myself to just settle in and remember that doubt and mental re-evaluation (of self and others) is a coping strategy for the Type 6—and their alertness to danger is a way to find safe alliances in an oft-appearing murky world.

Perhaps my favorite bird example of this is one of our pasture resident birds—the killdeer (*Charadrius vociferous*). A member of the plover family, many an unsuspecting hiker has been duped by the killdeer's "broken wing" behavior. I would love to translate into language what the killdeer is calling as she frantically limps across the path when intruders unwittingly encroach upon, what was once, her *idyllic* nesting site.

Her frantic bird call is accompanied by histrionic displays of fake-injury to lure the "threat" away from her black-and-white speckled eggs. Sadly, for the killdeer family, I fear that many of us don't fall for it—and instead just chuckle as we peer around the short grasses to find the clutch of eggs.

Like the SP-6, I perceive that this *dear bird* lives in a type of chronic anxiety—doubting himself and then doubling down on the doubts; leading to a sense of constant ambivalence. This push-pull behavior of the SP-6 and the killdeer, the "please you/test you" dance, can be truly and utterly exhausting.

Migration Flyway: From Indecision to Certainty

In a perceived dangerous world, the SP-6 seeks protection from others, and thus forms alliances. They become uncertain of their own authority and can appear a bit "flighty" as they ask a lot of questions, answer few, and have some difficulty making decisions. The SP-6 is insecure at the core, striving to be friendly and supportive; and in doing so, places a stigma on anger and aggression (their own and others). Thus, even more critical than taking risks, is the confidence that this individual will gain by owning his anger and expressing confidence when stating opinions. As with the killdeer, the SP-6 believes her anxiety is justifiable—when instead, the better plan will be to recognize that the impending danger may not, in fact, be "real" and that all of the kerfuffle may do more harm than good—that all of their ultra-preparedness, ultimately, prevents them from the act of doing.

TYPE 6, SOCIAL SUBTYPE (SOCIAL-6): AUTHORITY

> *I pray to the birds because they remind me of what I love*
> *rather than what I fear. And at the end of my prayers,*
> *they teach me how to listen.*
> Terry Tempest Williams

Precise. Dutiful. Loyal. For the Social-6, protection comes with allegiance to authority. Playing by the rules is the security net for this six, and anxiety is replaced by dogma. In the face of questionable circumstances, Social-6s want to know the rules, who are the *good* peeps and the *bad* peeps; this quells their steady hum of anxiety about impending peril.

I learned this via a very social chickadee as she nervously perched on a cedar branch, turned furtively and flew to the dangling potted geranium, and back again to the cedar.

Really? Does the deck outside my sister's condo truly seem dangerous? No lurking cats, no waiting falcons ready to dive bomb the little chick. Okay, okay, I confess, thirty minutes prior to this display of high-anxiety, I had moved her long-owned, mortgage-free geranium pot nest to a new and (in my humble opinion) improved location just one window box away. Yes! With a much better view and access to an above-ground "saucer-pool." But this dutiful, precise, feathered Social-6 home-owner was not pleased.

The Social-6 has an extreme intolerance for ambiguity, and similar to our little chickadee's coloring, sees the world in terms of black or white; not shady gray. This individual adheres to a life rulebook as their authority, and in this way overcomes her ever-present anxiety. Just follow the guidelines and all will go swimmingly.

Lest this Social-6, chickadee-house metaphor remain unclear, I had changed the HOA rules, thereby earning the title of a shady gray "bad peep." In defense of my outwardly heartless action, I was unable to explain to my downy tenant that her geranium-sublet was in serious need of a renovation; thus the forced relocation. Fortunately, after adequate observation and perching to gain various perspectives, my feathered friend warily entered her new nesting box. And I, sweating profusely and riddled with guilt, felt incredibly relieved with my renewed assignation as an upstanding proprietor.

Migration Flyway: From Authority to Intuition

Like the Social-6, many birds anticipate threats around every corner; the most benign experiences seem risky. Admittedly, some bird fears are, in fact, rational; call them cats! To our average tweety, it would be foolish *not* to fear; it is a protective instinct. Fear is what keeps us from diving into turbulent waters, or driving a car with no brakes. The key for the Social-6 is to come to peace with the fact that to live is to encounter the unexpected, then using intuition to discern when fear is rational or leading us astray.

TYPE 6, ONE-TO-ONE SUBTYPE/COUNTERTYPE: FEROCITY

Some birds are more willing than others
to take risks. It is well known that nuthatches
are among the less fearful of wild birds.
Joan Gibb Engel, *Taking the Auspices*

Strong. Intimidating. Risk-taker. For readers familiar with the Enneagram, these three words evoke the energy of a Type 8; the gut-driven protector. Surprise! These words more aptly describe the motivations of the One-to-One Type Six, the individual who prefers to fly into the turbulence and storm winds rather than draft or lie low.

In his book, *The Wisdom of Insecurity*, Alan Watts makes an eloquent case that life, by its very nature (and I add here, *within* nature) is uncontrollable. The point he emphasizes is that, in order to truly live life in the fullest sense, we need to stop trying to finalize our comfort and security, and instead, learn to navigate and accept a life that is rife with unpredictable changes. He goes further to suggest that human suffering comes from fighting this truth.

Watts writes, "Running away from fear *is* fear, fighting pain *is* pain, trying to be brave is *being scared.* If the mind is in pain, the mind is pain. The thinker has no other form than his thought. There is no escape." By my reading of this, we become what we focus upon and manifest the very thing we are trying our darndest to avoid. And while we are busy ruminating on the fears and anxieties surrounding our uncertain futures, we miss living life to its fullest. While we are planning all of the *what ifs,* we are missing the *here* and *now.*

The One-to-One 6 not only received this memo, she is determined to ignore the fear; instead this 6 turns *against* threats by confronting them head-on. Vastly different than the SP-6 Subtype, this bird steels her wings and flies into risk, confronting rather than shying away from danger. There is a multitude of evidence and specific examples of risk-taking among birds. In a 2017 article in the *Journal of Behavioral Ecology*, "Male risk-taking is related to number of mates in a polygynous bird," Bobby Habig and colleagues suggested that evolutionary theory predicts that when intrasexual competition is intense, risky bird behaviors can evolve, especially when they serve to enhance reproductive success. Basically, reinforcing the old adage, "the things we do for love"—in the avian world.

Being one that takes a "chill pill" on every airline flight, I've no earthly or heavenly idea regarding the high-risk mindset of the One-to-One Type 6 as they hang-glide off of cliffs or swim with sharks. My first thought is, *What* the * are you thinking? The word on the street is that by facing their fears they gain the sense of safety they seek. They use intimidation as a well-honed defense system against danger. So, this is their explanation? Fine. I'm still not bungee jumping. Just say'n.

Migration Flyway: From Ferocity to Vulnerability

I'm going to suggest an extreme attitude shift for the One-to-One Type 6: disarmament. With the armor removed, this 6 can feel their skin again, plus the vulnerability of exposing their fears. Then things get real. To paraphrase Brené Brown, to be vulnerable is the risk the One-to-One 6 must take to experience connection. Or, in poetic words:

> *He is not afraid of the wind, though he is cautious.*
> *He watches the snake, that stripe of black fire, until it flows away.*
> *He watches the hawk with her sharpest shins,*
> *aloft in the high tree.*
> *He keeps his prayer under his tongue.*
> *In his whole life he has never missed the rising of the sun.*
> Mary Oliver, "Catbird"

There is a seeming unpredictability about birds that, while exhilarating for some, may prove baffling and downright unnerving for others; especially those who prefer a more predictable existence. Given that the Type

6 birder is continually plagued with doubt and questions, this can pose a bird-watching conundrum. While we all long for some predictability, especially in our current world where a certain level of chaos seems to have become the status-quo, the Type 6 trumps us all in their *need to know.* And in nature, the bottom line is, we can plan on some consistency but must be prepared for the sudden change and downright shift in whatever plan you thought you had.

Only when we are no longer afraid do we begin to live.

Despite the bravado, the One-to-One Type 6 will benefit from being more vulnerable; to recognize and touch her fears. When I was diagnosed with Multiple Sclerosis in 2005, a friend said to me, *Breathe in hope and breathe out fear.* This was a vital message for me at that time, and a daily prompt for all One-to-One Type 6s: acknowledge the worries and hopes swirling in your heads, and choose hope; when beauty and ugliness mingle, cling to beauty. As their gentle Type 7 wing-man would remind them, when faced with despair and possibility, pursue endless possibilities.

TYPE 6 NAVIGATION TIPS

- Find the break in the nimbus clouds and let the sun shine in.
- Trust your compass's true north for self-confidence, and certainty.
- You can be loyal to your flock and still take a solo flight.
- Limit your web searches related to flight disasters (or similar catastrophic topics).
- Try to distinguish between kerfuffles, disasters, and free-flight anxiety.
- Find a quiet perch to quiet your anxious mind.
- Try not to second-guess your flight patterns.
- Not everything is a cautionary *tail* (feather).

A heart without dreams is like a bird without feathers.
Suzy Kassem

TYPE 7
THE JOYFUL BIRDER

ADVENTUROUS. VISIONARY. JOYFUL. If Type 7s had it their way, there would be all clear, blue skies ahead with ever-changing cloud patterns. The sky is actually not the limit for these birders—if they could they'd venture beyond; and in their minds, they likely do. Gluttony is the passion for all Type 7s, and while a bird lover of some other Type is lamenting that he only has one bird in the hand, the Type 7 will simultaneously be enticing hundreds into the bush. To know a Type 7 is to appreciate abundance and possibility.

If you have ever had a bucolic travel moment ruined, you will appreciate this story. I can still vividly recall the moment when we were preparing to board our tender boat to head out to one of the most remarkable natural places on our planet—the Galapagos Islands. Our small group of fifteen travelers and guides were lost in our thoughts, watching the pelicans and seagulls dive into the clear, crystal-blue waters of the Pacific. It was a rare and meaningful sip of tranquility, which some of us had dreamt about for years when seemingly out of nowhere one of our group members (definitely *not* Type 7) loudly exclaimed, "When they dive like that the little ones (pelicans) break their necks!"

SCA-REEECH!

Re-recording please!

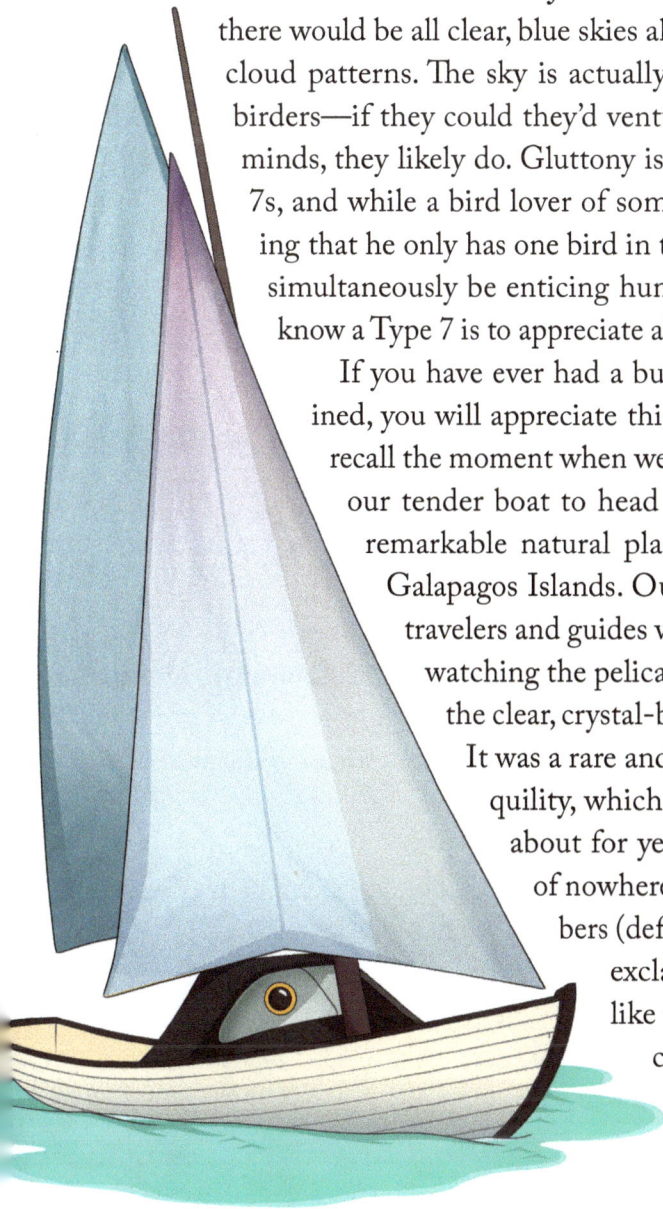

I admit that my first thought was to immediately scan my surroundings for the flotsam of dead baby pelicans. Upon seeing none in imminent danger, I rapidly made a mental note to stay as far away as humanly possible from this "downer" member of our motley travel group. And wow, was I *spot on*; she later complained about her blisters and maintained that "socks" were *not* on the suggested travel item list. Huh? It certainly does take all kinds to fill the planet.

Why am I featuring this story for the adventurous Type 7? Because I firmly believe that this experience is familiar to our Type 7 friends. Just when they hit their visionary-stride, some unsuspecting realist slams on the proverbial brakes. When the Type 7 has raised her billowing sail, caught a gust of wind, and yells, "blue skies ahead!" some pragmatist shares the storm forecast. Such a bummer. To Type 7s I fear we are all "downers" to their upward mobility; when they are soaring, we announce the headwinds ahead.

A wondrous bird is the pelican.
His mouth can hold more than his belly can.
He can take in his beak, enough food for a week!
I'll be damned if I know how the hell-he-can!

Dixon Lanier Merritt

How do Type 7s cope? I believe that for Type 7s, staying in moments of apprehension is so emotionally expensive and consumes so much energy that they allow themselves to grow numb to them to diminish them.

Read on to discover more about the Enneagram's visionary bird lovers. And one more note before I complete this section. During my five days on the Galapagos Islands I did not spot even one baby pelican in distress; although come to think of it, I didn't see *any* baby pelicans. Believe me; I know what you are thinking. Let's just put that thought to rest and channel our optimistic Type 7 energy, shall we?

Birds will give you a window, if you allow them.
They will show you secrets from another world—
Fresh vision that, though it is avian, can accompany you
home and alter your life.
They will do this for you even if you don't know their names—
though such knowing is a thoughtful gesture.
They will do this for you if you watch them.
Lyanda Lynn Haupt, *Rare Encounters with Ordinary Birds*

TYPE 7 FLOCK CHARACTERISTICS

- I want to see *all* of the birds you have seen and then see them again.
- I take great pleasure in many life experiences.
- I cultivate bird-loving buddies.
- I imagine the best possible experiences and ultimate (*insert word*).
- I get bored with the routine birding experiences such as *waiting to maybe see a bird.*
- I think some people take their birding way too seriously.
- I'd much rather anticipate something than finish it—I'm on to the next idea.
- Variety, spontaneity, and fun are the only ways to bird.
- I am into the best imaginable experience!

If these phrases resonate, you might identify as a Type 7 birder.

TYPE 7, SELF-PRESERVATION SUBTYPE (SP-7): SELF-SATISFYING

One cannot write a book about birds without mentioning their food-nemesis, squirrels. I have a rather grudging admiration for them. I cannot help but respect their stamina as I observe their rapid and tireless transport of the fallen pecans from beneath our bountiful tree (*was* bountiful, pre-squirrel annihilation), across the fence line, to various burrows surrounding our yard. And you cannot convince me that you haven't, at least once in your life, been in awe of the extreme acrobatics of squirrels as they repeatedly contort their sinewy, furry bodies to get a mouthful of birdseed. And yes, I, like every birder and gardener, cuss and fume through my secret admiration.

Similar to our hedonistic, frisky squirrel population, the SP-7 is often described as the epicure of the Enneagram Types. These folks make alliances, fraternal networks (squirrely friendships?) to meet their self-interests. Sound nuts to you? Keep reading. The SP-7s are very, *very* good at getting what they want and will go to extraordinary means to get it, including calculating and/or pragmatic means. If birds are the acrobats of nature's circus, squirrels are the ring leaders; together, the Cirque du Soleil of the natural world. So, *step right up*, just guard your popcorn!

Migration Flyway: From Self-satisfying to Self-aware

I always thought my bird-loving father was self-aware, until the day my mother told me that he was spray-painting squirrel tails. By way of explanation, he was trapping the birdseed-stealing rodents (see: Latin word *rodere*, meaning to gnaw), spraying their tails, and moving them to the local golf course. Obviously, the paint was not a fashion statement but to note if the same (did I say *damn*?) squirrels were returning to his bird-yard habitat. In his defense, the squirrels lived. I share this story not to paint my father as a nut, but to suggest that the SP-7 must move away from hedonistic behavior to the golf course! Nah!

This individual will benefit from recognizing that her materialistic tendencies are masking deeper feelings; and ultimately interfering with the pursuit of life goals.

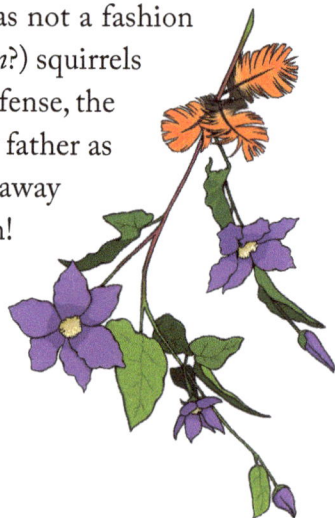

TYPE 7 SOCIAL SUBTYPE/ COUNTERTYPE (SOCIAL-7): SACRIFICE

Birds make great sky circles
of their freedom.
How do they do it?
They fall, and falling,
they're given wings.

Rumi

Sacrificial and helpful, the Social-7 is, by nature, a bird of a different color. Appearing similar to a Type 2 or 4, these individuals express a counter stance to gluttony by serving the greater good as social idealists. Let's take a social, ecological perch to view the avian Social-7s. Hands (and feathers) down, birds improve our human quality of life, psychologically and physically. Birds are mood boosters, whether summoning us to the call of the pileated woodpecker, or startling us with the otherworldly call of a cactus wren. Like service-minded Social-7s, birds make big contributions across habitats so that people and our planet continue to thrive. Take, for example, the soaring swallows ingesting multitudinous insects, rescuing pest-prone crops, and securing more food for us. And the next time you take a long hike and don't trip over a decomposing deer or rodent, you might want to silently thank a vulture. Scientists have noted that without vultures, carcasses take three times the standard to decompose, creating higher risk of disease for humans. While these bird behaviors may be more instinctual than the self-sacrificing ego motivation of the Social-7, the outcomes are much the same: a giving-back goodness for all.

Migration Flyway: From Sacrifice to Mindfulness

The Social-7 has a solid, pure motivation to give a lot rather than take it all; to be of service and diminish suffering. Quite the tall order from this writer's perspective. Folks of this Subtype will become even more *conscientious* when they become more *conscious* of their true motives, assuring that their anti-gluttonous acts aren't a facade to mask their underlying fears.

TYPE 7, ONE-TO-ONE SUBTYPE: IDEALIST

Birds, much like the One-to-One Type 7, allow us to be boundless, if only for a while; they provide the conduit for our imagination to run wild. For this Subtype of 7, every bird from the Gila woodpecker to the great blue heron may be a "spark bird," defined as the bird that helped spark your interest in birding, a bird that opens one's eyes to the incredible beauty, mystery, and passion of birding. For the idealistic, optimistic One-to-One Type 7, every single bird lights a positive fire; and the 7s spark-away! Akin to the optimism of someone who is in love, the One-to-One 7 idealizes every bird and human sighting, whether a scarlet tanager or a stranger on a train, as a way to avoid deeper emotions which might be unpleasant. Much like the plumage of the stunning, pink spoonbill, this birder is using *roseate*-colored binoculars. Pun aside, the sky is actually *not* the limit for the fervent imaginings of this Type.

This individual lives life as it could be, and sees every bird as they imagine them in some Eden, rather than some boring, urbane reality. When a Type 7 feels imprisoned by life's circumstances, birds provide an escape route. When One-to-One 7s feel utterly grounded, birds give them, and perhaps all of us, permission to fly.

> *Birds remind us to look up when our spirits are low. To take flight when we feel grounded. With a pair of wings and a destination—birds remind us of what is possible.*
> Angela M. Rosenberg

In her book, *Wintering*, Katherine May describes the robin as the "cheerleader of the bird family." She writes: "[Robins appear] when you are 'at low ebb' as if to encourage you onwards by reminding you that there is some magic left in the world."

I've often thought of Type 7s as magical beings, as they seem to exist in a plane just above the rest of us mortals, beckoning us to not be so *inflexible*, so *dogged*; instead to join them *above it all* in friendlier skies. I mean, what human or bird in their right mind begins chirping in the middle of the gloomy, cold, dark days of winter? Clue: they have a rich orange-colored breast; and I'm writ'n about the bird at the moment. The optimistic li'l robin, just singing his heart out in the middle of January, with his intelligent, cocked head as if to say to me, what's up with you, Ms. Downer? Robins are downright chipper—as they gluttonously dig up worm after worm. They remind us to believe that the world is bountiful, so we should all get about the business of appreciating and reap all there is on offer.

The One-to-One Type 7 is in sync with the robin (no, *not* digging up worms) as a type of human-omen, chiding us all to snap out of our doldrums and fly into the realm of our imagination. One-to-One Type 7s are known to, let's just say, embellish the human existence a bit, and, like the robin singing his complex song in the darkest days of winter, encourage us to imagine something better than any stark reality we are experiencing.

Migration Flyway: From Idealist to Realist

Unclose your mind. You are not a prisoner. You are a bird in flight, searching the sky for dreams.
Haruki Murakami

Some Enneagram scholars suggest that the One-to-One Type 7 is unconsciously over-compensating in order to avoid the sadness and pain that comes with the territory of being human. Perhaps. But I must admit, while this cynical Type 2 can occasionally find the One-to-One 7's unbridled enthusiasm annoying, it is an infectious annoyance! As bucolic and enticing as a 7-world can be, there is reality to face: bills, chores, jobs. Fine, hate me, but unless you were somehow born into a perpetual Eden, it's true for you, too. The One-to-One 7s need to come down to earth, and explore their need to embellish rather than face their true feelings.

TYPE 7 NAVIGATION TIPS

- Earth to 7's: Come down!
- You cannot fly in every direction at once. Choose one and stick to it.
- Overweight birds are grounded, limit your seed consumption.
- A little sadness makes the gladness all the better.
- Embrace your winter plumage, constant color is not realistic.
- No one likes a perpetual cheerleader; channel a wee bit of cynicism.
- If the sky is an unchanging blue, you will never experience the power of storm clouds.
- See Type 6: There *is* such a thing as a cautionary *tail* (feather).

We must be willing to get rid of the life we've planned,
so as to have the life that is waiting for us. The old skin
has to be shed before the new one can come.
Joseph Campbell

A Note on Molt

TRAIN YOUR BINOCULARS to the treetops in late Summer to see one of the most startlingly gorgeous birds you will ever witness—the male scarlet tanager. You might hear his raspy call that will signal you to his presence—then scan the treetops for a glimpse of his blood-red cape and dark black wings. I cannot resist appropriating a British Royal title to this striking passerine bird, (Prince) Piranga olivacea, of the Family Cardinalidae. Don't miss this sighting as he will soon molt and migrate to his winter forest palace in South America.

The concept of molting is a natural process of a bird's life cycle and consists of shedding the old and welcoming new, stronger feathers (often of a different color). This *letting go,* is not only natural, it is *essential* to a bird's existence as he can then fly more efficiently, safely, and stay insulated against the elements. A particular bird's plumage is adapted for its habitat/environmental conditions with various types of birds replacing feathers for different reasons and seasons. Some birds will keep their basic plumage (same color) all year and others will molt and transform their feather hue to an alternate breeding plumage.

At this point in your reading you are perplexed, re-checking the title of this book, fearing you inadvertently picked up a book on *Bird Molt*; but fear not, as I am simply making a case for you to molt via the Enneagram. Like birds, humans need to *molt* to enhance or bolster core personality qualities to become a more robust, vivid version of themselves or in contrast, to become more subdued. As with the birds, an individual may then *appear* to be a different *classification* or a hybrid version of himself for protection or resilience—while retaining his own, core unique personality characteristics.

The Enneagram provides us with a means to embrace this concept via Wings and Arrows/flyways, the potential to layer and weave dimensional characteristics with features of our core personality. To reiterate, our core Enneagram Type remains solid; once crowned Prince Scarlet, always Prince Scarlet. However, a wise bird knows when it is time to discard his worn, un-useful plumage and embrace a different hue. Similar to other migrating birds, the Prince has a need to—and at times, an urgency to—molt in order to survive and thrive.

TYPE 8
THE PASSIONATE BIRDER

*Some birds are
not meant
to be caged,
that's all.
Their
feathers are
too bright, their
songs too sweet
and wild.*

Stephen King

WILL. DRIVE. STRENGTH. There are some songs where I find myself cranking up the volume and fancying myself a young Annie Lennox; lusty songs where the drums seem to increase the power of my heartbeat. I title this group as my Type 8 songs; they empower me to feel like a prizefighter, ready to take on any challenger, be they friend or foe. "Solsbury Hill," written by Peter Gabriel, is undoubtedly one of those songs for me. With spiritual mastery, he shares a powerful moment in his life, when he climbed Solsbury Hill and an eagle appeared to him heralding a time for change—a winged teller of his future transition. Knowing his life was in a rut, he listened to the message of that eagle, his heart going Boom! Boom! Boom! telling him it was time to take a different path in life.

As a Type Two, this song feels at once foreign and prophetic for me. I play Solsbury Hill when I intuitively feel it is time to embrace my power and stop living out some pre-determined destiny. When I need to parachute out of the relational-plane and take an instinctual leap into the void, lifted by the currents and message of the eagle, my heart going Boom! Boom! Boom! This is but one of the many lessons the Type 8 has to teach the rest of us: not to worry what others may think, or to over-think oneself into inaction; to "go with our gut."

Using archetypical descriptors, Type 8s are strong, powerful, and generally speak their minds. They come by these traits honestly, as many Type 8s are raised to avoid weakness. Their responsibility is to protect themselves and also act on behalf of others.

The three Subtypes of Type 8 express the passion of *lust* in three distinct ways. The 8-Self-Preservation Sub-type goes for what is needed to survive in a powerful, lusty way; the Social-8 has a need to protect others and go up against those who might commit injustices, and the One-to-One 8 is a passionate and charismatic character who goes against social conventions in a provocative way.

For many readers, the instinctual, powerful energy of the Type 8 evokes vertiginous images of spiraling falcons, hawks, and eagles. Granted, raptors do represent a strong and bold presence in the world, but to my taste these birds seem to label the Type 8, which I am loath to do.

Marty, my husband of twenty-six years and a Type 8, provided me with some advice about the Type 8 bird assignation; he suggested that I not assign the blue jay, oft perceived as a brash bully bird, as the Type 8 icon. He shared that this choice would add "bird-shame" to what he perceives as an already stigmatized Type. Bummer. The startling blue jay is a strong and clever bird that doesn't shy away from conflict. That noted, his declaration, and many other comments I have received, speak to the notion that most people do not like to be stereotyped—even if with a bird designation!

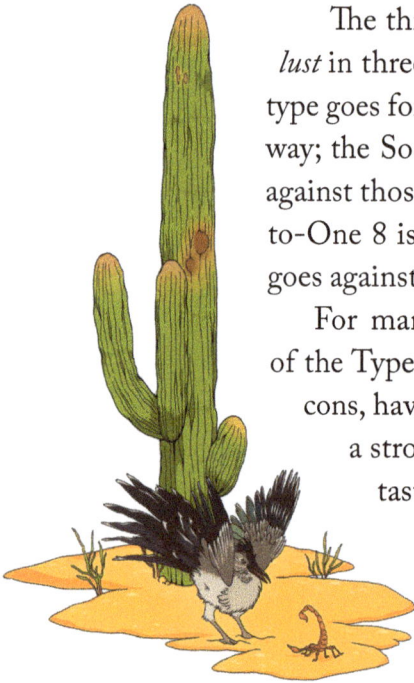

TYPE 8 FLOCK CHARACTERISTICS

- I don't have much respect for people or birds that don't stand up for themselves.
- Don't beat around the bush—I prefer direct communication.
- I make decisions fast, based on my instinctive bird-gut.
- I respect birds that migrate through tough conditions.
- A good debate serves to energize me!
- I am known for my tough feathers and talons.
- I step up and will take care of what needs to be done.
- Don't mess with me, the people I love, or my flock.

If these phrases resonate with you, then you might be a Type 8.

TYPE 8, SELF-PRESERVATION SUBTYPE (SP-8): SATISFACTION

I want to think again of dangerous and noble things. I want to be light and frolicsome. I want to be improbable beautiful and afraid of nothing, as though I had wings.

Mary Oliver

The self-preservation instinct is a biological drive directing energy toward safety and security; many of us have experienced this feeling at one time or another. The SP-8 is a no-nonsense type of person, easily frustrated when not getting his/her needs met. Societal norms are more of a suggestion than an obligation, and will be disregarded for this person to get what he wants. A straightforward individual, the SP-8 knows how to gain advantage to get what he wants. Many individuals of this 8 Subtype view themselves as survivors, and they are bound and determined to go to great lengths to get what they desire.

    I had a significant birding self-preservation moment perched on a craggy outcrop overlooking the Pacific Ocean in Patagonia, Chile, one of a small group of birdwatchers on the lookout for a tiny, highly motivated, yellow-eyed penguin. This particularly brave penguin, like the SP-8, is a survivor who will go to great lengths to meet his own and the needs of his family.

Our small band of travelers crouched, still as statues, seven total strangers with one thing in common—our desire to spot this elusive creature. We could hear him making his slow, perilous ascent, mainly due to the sound of falling pebbles and rocks—the male yellow-eyed penguin, returning diligently to his rocky cave, where two fuzzy chicks awaited his return with wide-open beaks. Our group had arrived early morning, and during the hour-plus vigil, our guide shared stories of the beautiful rituals of the long, life-mating pair of yellow-eyed penguins: the female and male alternately journey out to sea for days, swimming against strong currents and evading predators, working hard to supply food for their hatch; and the other one remains, attentive to the safety and security of the chicks during the mate's absence. At some point over the course of our *watch*, we began to assume collective responsibility for the fate of those defenseless chicks. Our guide impressed upon us that even our tiniest movement could disturb "our" male penguin's return to the cave and his hungry brood. In a few short hours, we had unwittingly joined our fierce penguin in a self-preservation bond to raise two vulnerable yellow-eyed chicks.

Migration Flyway: From Satisfaction to Vulnerability

The SP-8 finds it difficult to express vulnerability. I recount a recent example when an SP-8 colleague of mine shared an argument he had had with a *former* friend over whether the brown lump in the ocean was a pelican or a block of wood; his money was on the block of wood. The debate was a stalemate; the holiday ended. End of vacation. End of relationship.

I said, "Seriously, you split over a pelican versus a block of wood? Wasn't there more to it?"

He couldn't recall.

I said, "You never back down from a good debate!"

He replied, "Why would I back down when I'm always right!" *(Wink wink.)*

You laugh. He's serious.

To grow, the SP-8 must recognize that allowing feelings to surface and manifest is at the heart of being human. In fact, the very feelings that SP-8s perceive as weakness are their path to great strength. The emotional wall that the SP-8 has constructed to care for himself is akin to selfishness, and the way to dismantle it is to admit that he, too, could embrace a bit of humility *(wink wink)*. And for the record, pelicans eventually *move*, wood doesn't.

TYPE 8, SOCIAL SUBTYPE/COUNTERTYPE (SOCIAL-8): GUARDIAN

Fiat justitia, ruat caelum.
Let there be justice, though the heavens fall.
Attributed to: Johannes Jacobus Manlius, Loci Communes

The Social-8s are all about justice and will strive to create a fair and equitable community for all. A wise Type 8 once shared her take on life, that some of us win the lottery of the womb; born into a life that seems, to observers, to garner them great advantage. She shared that her mission in life was to work for equity, for all. Moreover, she believed that while her work and decisions may not always be accurate, she strives to be fair. This sentiment describes the Social-8 in a nutshell. The Countertype of the three 8 Subtypes, the Social-8 is a helpful person, appearing loyal and less aggressive. This is a bird with protective feathers of a slightly different color, edged in sensitivity, aimed toward righting the wrongs inflicted upon others.

Having just returned from a trip to Egypt, I was struck by how the indomitable qualities of Horus, the falcon god, represent characteristics of the Social-8. Horus was a revered god in the form of a falcon whose right eye represented the sun/morning star, quintessence, and left eye, the moon/evening star, representing healing. Symbolically Horus is similar to the Social-8, a child who is thought to have become tough to protect the mother against patriarchal power. According to this myth, prominent about 2350 BCE, Horus was born to Osiris and Isis and was the nephew of Seth (depicted as a crocodile), Osiris's brother. The story 'round Egypt is that Seth murdered Osiris, and contested Horus's heritage. If you aren't into Egyptian mythology you might note the similarities in the *Lion King*, starring li'l Simba as a Social-8. Now, back to Egypt: Horus became Seth's enemy and eventually defeated Seth, avenging his father, Osiris, and he assumed the throne. During this act of violence, born of solidarity and protection, Horus lost his left eye, the moon. This is a bummer; however, Horus the falcon god is now depicted as an eye with a tear—signifying protection, health, and restoration.

While most Social-8s don't engage in this type of outward violence, they do typically lose perspective regarding their own needs for care and protection; instead looking out for those who are least able to defend themselves.

Migration Flyway: From Guardian to Beneficiary

To express vulnerability and a need to be cared for is extremely difficult for all of the 8 Subtypes. The Social-8, the Countertype of the 8s, appears to have a softer, calmer demeanor than the One-to-One or SP Subtype; but like Horus, he has a blind spot when it comes to recognizing his own needs for protection and loving care. The message for the Social-8 is to lean on his Type 9 Wing—draft a while, rely on the flock to meet his needs. There is a great lesson for the Social-8 in allowing others to reciprocate the care and love Social-8s bestowed upon them; others then gain a sense of their own agency rather than a dependency.

TYPE 8, ONE-TO-ONE
SUBTYPE: INDOMITABLE

You were once wild, don't let them tame you.
Isadora Duncan

The incomparable Isadora Duncan danced her way across the world creating an art form that was untamed, wild, and free. She said that her inspiration was drawn "from trees, from waves, from clouds, from the sympathies that exist between passion and the storm, between gentleness and the soft breeze." Duncan strove to connect movement with emotion—"seeking that dance which might be the divine." Following her advice, we can draw wisdom from the strong and passionate One-to-One Type 8.

Outspoken and flying against the norm, this Subtype is the most rebellious of the three Type 8 Subtypes, and yet, surprisingly, the most emotional. Possessing a strong anti-social tendency, the One-to-One 8 earns a reputation for being pugnacious, so don't be startled when this individual steps (strides!) up to share what's not going in the direction he feels is "just." While some find this behavior unreasonably argumentative, to the One-to-One 8 a confrontational stance is energizing, and this individual feels most alive when fully engaged with others in defense of his values. In actuality, it is a matter of pride for this Subtype to fly against the flock. This individual conveys energetic, charismatic energy, and not only can, but will dominate her environs. In the avian world, many a raptor conveys the spirit of this Subtype: hawks, eagles, falcons. However, the One-to-One 8, given his intensity and solitary nature, summons a particular bird for me: the "fisher-king."

It's October in the low country of South Carolina, and the belted kingfishers are on the move. Their piercing, staccato rattle is unmistakable as they fly, with Arrow-like intensity, across sun-dappled fall marsh grasses toward their eventual plunge into the

Folly River. Like the One-to-One 8, fascinating and charismatic, the belted kingfisher embodies a type of seductiveness, a watchful intensity. Unlike the other two 8 Subtypes, this Subtype exudes a distinctive panache. The female belted kingfisher, with her stylish cap and chestnut neck scarf, shows her magnetic color, especially when hovering over the sparkling river, bathed in sunlight, the star of her own Broadway show. This bird, like the One-to-One 8, has an air of self-importance as she patrols up and down rivers and shorelines, nesting in burrows along earthen banks. This One-to-One bird will not often be mistaken for another species, given she is an indomitable *force de la nature*.

Migration Flyway: From Indomitable to Accepting

Vulnerability is the safest flight path for the One-to-One Type 8; this *tough ol' bird* must molt, trading provocation for pluck. Insight for this Subtype 8 is recognizing that exposing the soft underbelly of her emotions will make for a stronger, more resilient migration. She must channel the spirit of Amelia Earhart as she embarked on her 1932 solo flight across the Atlantic in her Lockheed Vega plane, Old Bessie, the fire horse. Did her heart race like a hummer when her engine sputtered as she glided over that mighty, deep, and endless ocean? When she encountered the fierce winds and thunderclouds, did she transcend her fears by embracing her iridescent wings? Many books and songs suggest she was a woman with immense courage, while others allude to her drive and competitive spirit; her relentless search for the next prize. My theory is that she accepted her vulnerabilities, and that knowledge infused her with resolve, with fortitude. I'll wager our winged-woman was a transcendent One-to-One Type 8, who understood and accepted her aerial vulnerability; her aeronautical success stories certainly support that theory.

TYPE 8 NAVIGATION TIPS

- Try moderation in one endeavor in life and nature.

- All matters aren't black-and-white—channel your inner yellow-eyed penguin.
- Don't ignore your emotions; they are as important as your gut.
- Big is not always better; in fact, the tiniest birds sing the prettiest songs.
- Birding is a quiet, reflective space, take note.
- Admitting weakness symbolizes great strength.
- Witness the fragility of a fledgling bird, the vulnerability of the avian world.

TYPE 9
THE PEACEFUL BIRDER

Everyone suddenly burst out singing;
And I was filled with such delight
As prisoned birds must find in freedom,
Winging wildly across the white
Orchards and dark-green fields; on - on - and out of sight.
Everyone's voice was suddenly lifted;
And beauty came like the setting sun:
My heart was shaken with tears; and horror
Drifted away, O, but Everyone was a bird;
and the song was wordless; the singing will never be done.

Siegfried Sassoon, "Everyone Sang"

"EVERYONE SANG" IS a beautiful poem that resonates with joy and peace. Those familiar with Sassoon's work and the time period during which he was writing will recognize that this poem is the speaker's reflection upon the end of World War I. The stanzas reflect the resurgence of communal joy and the dissipation of the horror the country had lived with for so long. I invite you to now embody this sense of peace and joy as we explore the flight patterns of the irenic Type 9. The message of the 9 for all of us is to fret less, compete less, control less, and overall to go a little easier on ourselves and others. Like soaring birds, Type 9s are seen as unflappable, skilled at conserving their energy to navigate life's changing winds.

I recently read the quote, "patience is an action, too," and immediately thought of Type 9s, known for their ability to embrace alternative perspectives and adopt a deliberate, unhurried pace. The latter qualities evoke an image of a great white egret, a type of heron, as an archetypical bird for the 9. When observing an egret or great blue heron at rest in a marsh, you may question if you have teleported to a sculpture garden, as a heron's overall countenance is remarkably still and unhurried. Whilst observing this remarkable bird, I suggest you settle down for a long linger, because, not unlike the calm Type 9, herons have a tendency to merge with the tall, willowy grasses and simply *wait* for the incoming tide. Ahhhh.

TYPE 9 FLOCK CHARACTERISTICS

- Birding is meant to be a peaceful pursuit, not a competition.
- When I feel pressured, my feathers may get ruffled.
- I need a little push to wake up with the birds—but once I get going, I appreciate the peace and quiet.
- I may appear more peaceful than I really am inside.
- Conflict—ugh! I prefer the flight path of least resistance.
- I opt to use "zone out" strategies instead of dealing with life—like watching *Winged Migration* for the fifth time.
- On a journey, I am much more likely to go along with whatever the group chooses, rather than force my own desires.
- Feeling pressured and rushed is truly *for the birds.*
- I work hard and may sacrifice my own agenda to support my team.
- I may waiver when it comes to making a final decision!

If these phrases resonate, you might identify as a Type 9 birder.

TYPE 9, SELF-PRESERVATION SUBTYPE (SP-9): COMFORT

I awoke and fell in love
Canada geese at dawn's first light
The call of a loon
Still lake at night
A newborn's touch
Sliver of moon

I fell in love
Not a moment too soon

Angela M. Rosenberg

If you find yourself in the presence of an SP-9, you may experience their sense of calm—and linger a while in their aura. The majority of SP-9s are practical people who tend to favor more quiet, alone-time than the other two 9 Subtypes. This SP-9 finds comfort in routine, be it bird-watching or other pursuits. They hunger for the simple things in life—fulfilling their physical needs in straightforward, simple ways.

I encountered one such individual when hired by a large biotech firm to coach several managers targeted for high-level leadership positions. At the onset of our first meeting, my client shared that, before we embarked on his executive coaching sessions, he had a confession to make.

To be clear, this type of statement strikes fear in the heart of every executive coach. My initial thought was to tell him, "Please don't say another word! Plead the Fifth." My follow-up thoughts, in swift succession, were: "Oh God, he is going to confess to embezzlement"; and "He murdered his former boss in Reno and watched him die." Unleashed, my mind was a slippery slope of flagrant transgressions by this seemingly kind and gentle man.

Instead he simply stated, "I've absolutely no aspiration to join the rat race of corporate leadership. I'd much prefer to be the 'Goose Guy.'" My initial feeling was one of immense relief; I needn't call the authorities or the IRS. My second thought may be similar to your own, "Who the hell is the *Goose Guy?*"

Much to my surprise, I was the one *schooled* that day, and will share the valuable lesson I learned about the motivations of an SP-9. Known for their desire for protection and comfort, the SP-9 tends to forget their *own being* and engage in comfortable activities and routines; avoiding the conflicts and over-stimulation that often come with erratic and combustible career positions. With this desire in mind, my new client then explained to me the role (I cannot bring myself to call what follows a *career*) of the *Goose Guy* (GG).

My client had been observing the GG during his daily breaks, where he relished the opportunity to sit on a bench at the edge of the impeccably manicured corporate-pond. On multiple occasions he spotted a kindred spirit—a lone man sitting at the pond edge with several dogs—who routinely harassed a number of Canada geese (the dogs, not the man). He would see the man and his trusty pups for several days in a row, until man, dogs, and geese abruptly disappeared. This pattern continued throughout the spring until my client finally inquired as to the reason for these sporadic, brief visits and subsequent long absences.

He shared that the gentleman responded as though his purpose should have been insanely obvious to the casual observer. He simply stated, "I am the *Goose Guy*"; hired to rid the manicured pond of the pesky Canada geese. The geese were not only aggressive with employees (I defended the geese here, interjecting that a pond *is kind of their space),* but they poop and molt around the pond, creating, well, a *big mess.* The Goose Guy is hired and paid quite handsomely to rid the pond of the geese; a basic "Goose-Be-Gone" business model. My client went on to explain that he had asked the Goose Guy the obvious question, "Where do the geese *go?*"

The Goose Guy replied, as if equally obvious, "To the *(name withheld) Corporate Headquarters* pond, about two miles down the road." At this point, the GG is called to rid *that* pond of the geese. And so it goes. This is the pattern of the storied career of the Goose Guy.

At this point my client recognized that this comfortable routine was the type of calling to which he aspired, *not* the corporate ladder. His true calling was to sit on the bank of a grassy pond, communing with nature, and nudging Canada geese to fly down the road. My coaching challenge was to find a way to get him compensated for this type of work because, evidently, the goose-gig was already taken.

I conjecture that Canada geese are Self-Preservation Type 9s. Did I pull this out of thin air, you ask? If you doubt, just look up when you hear the honks emanating from a wedge of Canada geese (as opposed to a *blizzard* of snow geese?) Please take note that, like SP-9s, these birds are classic drafters; and there is, indeed, a reason for their V-shaped flight pattern. The majority of the Canada geese assume a V-formation to take advantage of the lift that each goose gets from the air moving over the wings of the goose ahead. In this way, the members of the formation can fly over 70 percent farther than if they flew alone. Talk about getting by with a little help from your friends, right?

I initially wondered how they decided upon this flight pattern (short feather draw, perhaps?) but it makes sense that the strongest flyers will take the lead. As a goose tires, he will fall back into the formation and another will take his place. It gets even better, as they communicate with clear signals! The members of the flock will honk to show they are doing well and the leaders should continue to fly rather than rest. I have taught executive leadership for over twenty-five years, and I never once considered telling company team members to honk to signal that they are in their groove. Move over Google, my new client is "Go-Goose" and I've got some new communication strategies to share with your management team.

Migration Flyway: From Comfort to Emergence

While all Type 9s distract themselves from their own sense of being, the SP-9 finds particular comfort in daily routine and activities. Regretfully, these rituals can literally keep them grounded, rather than risking exploration of uncharted self-terrain. And the beat goes on, day after day, year after year. The SP-9 habituates to this ostensibly safe solo flight, zoning out with habitual activities rather than people.

In migration, SP-9s can follow the path of their virtue, *right action*. This term is described in the literature as the one act that is of the *heart's knowing, that one unstoppable thing*. When the SP-9s wake up, they recognize the need to leave the safe nest of their knowing and enter the fray, the messiness of life with the flock, to truly find inner and outer peace.

TYPE 9, SOCIAL SUBTYPE/COUNTERTYPE (SOCIAL-9): ENGAGEMENT

We go through life. We shed our skins. We become ourselves.
Patti Smith

The Social-9 Subtype tends to disperse their immense energy outward instead of focusing on their own agenda. The bird perching on their burden-laden shoulder sings, *you need to earn your existence through hard work; take one for the team*. And this Subtype, the Countertype of the Type 9, responds by working incredibly hard to support the group's agenda; to feel included. Unlike their Type 2 look-alike, who often leads with a stripe of pride on the wing, the Social-9 presents with feathered humility, leaving their ego on a high branch. Adopting an organizational lens, this individual exhibits many of the qualities of a "servant leader," a leadership philosophy that emerged in the 1970s that is based upon core key concepts of Robert K. Greenleaf, related to spiritual insights and humility. Similar to the underlying focus of attention of the Social-9, the goal of the servant leader is to fly among, not above, their flock. This individual seeks to be one with the group and puts forth extreme effort to ensure everyone is heard and conflict is avoided. This 9 Subtype is a selfless person, who works very hard to accomplish the goals and needs of the group. To fit-in is critical, so this person will strive to be lighthearted, generous, and self-sacrificing.

Enter the cedar waxwing as the bird exemplar for the Social-9. If you think of the cedar waxwing as the burglar of the bird world, hanging from the branch above with his black mask and multicolored cape,

you might be inclined to check your pockets for
fear that you've been mugged. How-
ever, you would be sorely mistaken.
Waxwings are, quite literally, vora-
ciously devouring berries to the point
of drunken bliss. And while some regard them as
a raucous flock, these colorfully nuanced birds are known
as *Peacemakers* in the bird community, their only claim to
looting being perfectly ripe berries.

To spot cedar waxwings, you must tune your senses to their humble
peep-peep sound and look for discarded food droppings from the tree
canopy. Look up and you will find a flock of these beauteous birds in a
juniper tree known to have delish berries. The remarkable aspect of waxwing behavior is how they know when the moment is right (or ripe) for
the pickin'; they map the terrain to literally find themselves in the berry-
laden yards or fields. Perhaps they borrow from their 6 Arrow, to plan,
prepare—extraordinaire.

As with the Social-9, it is rare to see one waxwing—instead you will
hear them fluttering among the berry-laden branches, perching and
working as servers on a seamless buffet line. Often these beautiful ban-
dits pass a berry back and forth, bill to bill, until one swallows; a practice
of mutually beneficial teamwork. So there you have it—I've given you an
"earful" of information about the cedar waxwing.

Migration Flyway: From Engaged to Egocentric

While there is great comfort in meeting the needs of the flock, for an individual of this Subtype, it is a distraction from the underlying feeling of
being an outsider. The Social-9 can fly to new heights when she becomes
more in touch with her own personal-development journey; do I dare say,
savor and swallow some berries before passing?

TYPE 9, ONE-TO-ONE SUBTYPE: FUSION

I lift my arms, fingers spread
And mold them to your wings
Feeling the tender beat of your heart
We rise effortlessly
At once one
Among the beckoning billowing clouds
Angela M. Rosenberg

A universal experience is that hearing a few notes of a particular melody can wind us back in time. I was just a bit past the "edge of seventeen" when I first heard Stevie Nicks of the iconic band, Fleetwood Mac, belting out the lyrics to a song that put the fairly unremarkable white-winged dove on the charts. And by the way, if you are of Boomer, Gen-X, or Millennial age, I can hear you cooing as you read this—*ooh-ooh-ooh*.

But unlike the charismatic lead singer, the One-to-One 9 Subtype prefers to sing back-up for *another band* member, rather than take center stage. A bird sweetheart, less assertive, gentle and kind, the One-to-One 9 prefers to fuse and merge with, and support, the lead singer rather than the whole band. This accompanist role fills the inner void and results in a harmony that appears to have no boundaries. Perhaps an individual of this 9 Subtype is more akin to Christine McVie, the understated Fleetwood Mac keyboardist, than Stevie.

In the winged version of Fleetwood Mac, you will find the white-winged dove milling around the backyard feeder, preferring to adopt the attitudes and stance of others, rather than assuming the spotlight. A simple coo (okay, *ooh*), will do, much like their close cousin the mourning-dove.

I vividly recall on one of my first trips to Costa Rica, the bird guide describing the call of the white-winged dove as *who cooks for you?* It seems clear that, given the collaborative, kind nature of the One-to-One 9, I suppose they will cook for all of us. Not to mention, they will cook what we like rather than what they would prefer to eat.

If you find yourself on a bird *meander* (9s meander while the rest of us *hike)* with a One-to-One 9, and you ask her what direction *she* wants to go, you will most likely get the response, "Whatever direction *you* want to go is fine by me." God forbid if you aren't sure, as this can begin a very circular conversation of "who's on first?" and you will never begin your hike. Your One-to-One 9 friend is quite happy to follow your lead; or in the bird world, nibble on *your* favorite seed, all day long. She has a strong desire to *be* through *you* rather than to find her own direction.

Migration Flyway: From Fusion to Uniqueness

The characteristic flight pattern for the One-to-One 9 is *fusion* with you or some *other*, when she would benefit from finding her own purpose in life. Lamentably, those of this Subtype find it more comfortable to follow others' feelings, attitudes, beliefs, and at times, behavior.

If only the One-to-One 9 could adopt a line from Sammy Davis Jr.'s popular 1960s ballad, "I Gotta Be Me" and discern her own path. Stevie Nicks might pose this question to the One-to-One 9: What's the song you should be singin': *Ooh, Ooh, who?* are *You, You, You?*

TYPE 9 NAVIGATION TIPS

- Recognize your birding zone-out strategies, and try to avoid them.
- Embrace your own opinions rather than merging with those of the flock.
- Frustrations and disagreements are not only healthy, but essential in true relationships.
- The spring birds are calling you; please respond before winter.
- Be the director of your own flight plan; don't allow others to make it for you.
- Take the direct bird trail. The passive-aggressive route is a dead end.

TYPE 1
THE CONSCIENTIOUS
BIRDER

Your legs will get heavy and tired.
Then comes a moment of feeling
the wings you've grown, lifting.
Rumi

RESPONSIBLE. THOROUGH. TIRELESS.
These are but a few of the words used to describe the improvement-focused Type 1. I doubt there is a birder that is more keenly aware of the impact of climate change on our bird habitats than the Type One. The natural gift of the Type 1 is to notice what is out of sync or in need of improvement—and set their sail to "fix it." In this regard, the health (or in many cases, demise) of bird habitats will be a keen focus for our Type 1s.

With this in mind, I considered the vulture as a potential Type 1 bird. Vultures have been viewed as "protectors" as far back as circa 3200 BCE, with the symbol of the predynastic Egyptian goddess, Nekhbet, depicted as the (griffin) vulture goddess. Protector of Upper Egypt, the vulture goddess's wings spread upward, representing a goddess of heaven, using her wings to protect the pharoah.

I reconsidered this choice out of pure cowardice—knowing many-a-One that would cease to be my friend if I associated their personality attributes to those of a vulture. However, this is the rare instance the Type 1 would be incorrect. Hence, I beg all Type 1 readers to hear me out and forgive the following vulturous-pecadillo.

Related to the stork, the vulture's scientific name in Latin means "cleansing breeze"; nature's avian recycler. Commonly seen in the southern United States, the turkey vulture is tirelessly and thoroughly cleaning up our roadsides and planet. They are indefatigable, diligent, and untiring.

Hmm. Does this description not have a striking resemblance to Type 1 characteristics?

I recently read this line in a newsletter and it speaks to my sentiment about vultures: *Human beings are neither vultures nor crows. The world would count itself lucky if we were vultures. An actual vulture turns death into feathers.* Consequently, I am calling on all 1s to guide us all in our efforts to protect our birds and revitalize our planet.

TYPE 1 FLOCK CHARACTERISTICS

- My binoculars are focused on what needs improvement.
- When I fly, I fly in the proper fashion.
- I often perceive what I can do better in all of my endeavors.
- I focus on modeling what I perceive to be the "right" way.
- I reflect upon how I could improve my birding skills.
- I like checklists and birding goals.
- I take backyard birding seriously.
- I do *not* enjoy criticism. I am already hard enough on myself.
- I strive to learn and practice habits to protect both native and migrating birds.
- Details are important to me and not to be overlooked.

If these phrases resonate, you might identify as an Enneagram Type 1.

TYPE 1, SELF-PRESERVATION SUBTYPE (SP-1): CONTROL

You can spot a Type 1 Self-preservation Subtype because they are the "one" that is up and out for the dawn chorus with their regional bird list (easily accessible) and cleaned, situated binoculars—FOCUS! And dare ye' non-1s chat or crunch leaves while hopping down the bird-spotting trail, you will likely receive a sideways glance from an SP-1 that speaks volumes (as in, *Shut the hell up, puhleeese*). This Subtype is self-controlled and focused on making sure everything is under control. Moreover, anger is the seed most buried. The SP-1's anger is transformed from hot fire to a warm glow. In this way, they can appear like a Type 6: leading with restrained control rather than anger. A self-composed disquiet.

Seeing themselves as highly flawed individuals, SP-1s are focused on *self-* rather than *other-* perfection. They are the true perfectionists of the Enneagram. If only a well-intentioned friend were to point out to the anxious-but-trying-not-to-show-it Type 1 that they aren't responsible for, well, *everything,* so it's ok to *chill out,* the SP-1 might be surprised. This is because her impulses and body language may very well be unconscious and the likely result of a long family history where chaos reigned.

> *I am only one, but I am one.*
> *I cannot do everything, but I can do something.*
> *And I will not let what I cannot do*
> *interfere with what I can do.*
> Edward Everett Hale

Migrate: From Control to Carefree

Expounding on the quote above, the SP-1 has a daily choice: to embrace a space for worry to drift above her or allow worry to nest in her head-space. To truly soar, the SP-1 must wing away from worry and migrate to the playful, less critical, free-style gliding of the Type 7. Turn down the continual self-critical voice in her head, and rise above it, winging toward pleasure and play. Don't we all truly long to see a hawk gliding above us, seemingly free of all worries? So, don't be afraid to glide awhile, beautiful SP-1; you'll be the envy of all who witness your new heights.

TYPE 1, SOCIAL SUBTYPE (SOCIAL-1): UNYIELDING

> *Let us temper our criticism with kindness.*
> *None of us comes fully equipped.*
> Carl Sagan

The Social-1 Subtype will "model the way" with the mantra: "My way is the flyway!" Being of a punctilious nature, this translates into a need to know and demonstrate the correct way to behave. Here's the deal: there is the way *it* is *currently* done and there is the *correct way* it *should be* done. The Social-1 defines the correct way and is at the ready to tell you how to basically "get with the program!" Equipped with this knowledge, individuals of this Subtype will quell their anger and attempt to use intellect to control your actions and nudge you toward enlightenment. This is the lifelong quest of the Social-1: to inform others; to bring us all *into the light*, to gift the world with more reassurance, clarity, and understanding.

The middle of my three nieces and her husband are devoted to the "red bird," the cardinal, as a harbinger of truth in their life together. Much like the Social-1, they believe that a cardinal will "show up" for them, especially when they seek clarity or affirmation related to their life choices. For many, to witness a cardinal represents a visit from the ancestors, conveying a spiritual or emotional sense of reassurance and protection. For me, the cardinal, with its striking plumage, is a profound reminder that remarkable beauty exists in the world if I simply pause and pay attention.

At the risk of all Social-1 Subtype readers getting smug from the get-go, Social-1 Types are *almost always* correct, with a third eye toward the betterment of us all. While that may be a secondary point to many readers, it is definitely not secondary to a Social-1. This sense of rectitude is the very reason these individuals continue to doggedly pursue improvement of the *milieux generale*; exhausting themselves and often those around them.

Migrate: From Unyielding to Flexible

> *Use what talents you possess; the woods would be very silent if no birds sang there except those that sang best.*
> HenryVan Dyke

My father, to whom this book is dedicated, used to say to me, "Straighten up and fly right," which basically meant to get *my act together*! This phrase comes from a 1943 song made famous by Nat King Cole. While the song is a whimsical tune about a buzzard and a monkey, the gist is clear: don't lose your cool, don't dip and dive—do it "right." The problem faced by the Social-1 is that, in contrast to these lyrics, she could gain a lot of mileage by employing some behavioral dips and dives; instead of imposing her version of "right" onto everyone else. This 1 desires to bring us all *into the light*, yet she will gain social mileage by gently placing twigs and straw in the cracks, allowing us all to find our own way in the darkness.

The Social-1 can benefit, in particular, by taking wing toward Type 7, to make alliances with others; recognizing that he doesn't have a monopoly on the flight plan.

TYPE 1, ONE-TO-ONE
SUBTYPE/COUNTERTYPE: FERVOR

The Type 1, One-to-One Subtype is the paragon of high-flying standards, having an idealistic view of how things should be and wants to point others toward the light. This Type 1 is easily irritated, and while trying to be cool, will get frustrated if their bird group is not up to speed with birding etiquette—and they *will* let you know. Heck, they would correct the birds' behaviors if they had a chance of succeeding! This birder will have little patience with bird group members who are loud talkers or stompers. Get with the bird-program or get off of the trail, would be their request. This individual has a need to perfect others and can be impatient and angry as they attempt to reform them. Contrary to the other, more repressed/controlled Type 1 Subtypes, this is the forceful individual that does not resist her desires, boldly displaying her impulsive, frustrated feathers. My image is of the fussy bird at the birdbath, stressing that the other "drinkers" must sip and savor, not gulp! Or any version of the video game, *Angry Birds*, ruffled feathers and all.

Migration Flyway: From Fervor and Zeal to Lightness of Being

In the words of the great moral philosopher and novelist, Iris Murdoch, this individual will reach new heights when she recognizes that *there are infinitely many kinds of beautiful lives; to step outside the self, beyond its particular conceptions of beauty—which includes, of course, moral beauty—and walk with humble, nonjudgmental curiosity about the myriad other selves afoot on their own paths, propelled by their own ideals of the Good.*

In lay terms, stop preening everyone; not your job, not your feathers! Things definitely go south when you decide that you get to create the guidelines for how other people live their lives. Draw your own lines, live your life by them, respect others' right to do the same. The flight will be much less turbulent. This One-to-One Subtype needs to tone it down a notch and tune into the fact that their virtuous intensity and self-interest is really messing with everyone else's mojo. Instead, this Type 1 can migrate to the Type 4 and channel her anger and desires consciously, by plumbing her own deeper motives. Wisdom can be gained by becoming fully present to the unfolding wonder of the world; letting go of the need to control the narrative. If only this Type 1 could envision the possibility of a more just and generous future ahead. This is an invitation to enjoy free flight.

> *What's true here is delight. What's true is the flight of a soul testing her wings and finding them air-worthy. What's true are all the many and self-judgments, challenges of life, from pain all arrayed like laundry on the line so I can decide which ones to fold and which get relegated to the rag pile. What's true here is a glorious day blown in on storm winds. What's true is the choice to be awake, alive, and joyous in the face of whatever this day brings. What's true is giving thanks and taking none of this for granted.*
> Danna Faulds

Type One Navigation Tips

- The "early bird (may) get the worm," but he'll also be exhausted.
- You can still fly high with lowered expectations of those around you.
- When your birding-critic whispers, tell it to take-a-*flight*.
- Lower the ceiling for yourself and those around you—the sky is hard to reach.
- The birds will sing tomorrow, so put those binoculars down for the day—and perhaps take some time to simply play.
- The bird you identified was a *Pyrrhuloxia* not a *Phainopepla*! So many Ps—so *do* forgive you.
- Birders (and humans) can be critical; try to take their feedback without it ruffling your feathers.
- Let go of your need to inform or perform—simply enjoy the journey.

CONCLUSION

IN LEADERSHIP COACHING, we advise that the best place to begin to understand others is to come to know oneself deeply. As a birder, this means beginning in your own backyard, be it a wooded forest, suburban park, city block, or pasture land. Attune yourself to the birdsongs and behaviors that surround you daily—the flutterings at your window, the skirmishes at your feeders. And when you recognize these birds as your neighbors, it is time to begin your own winged migration!

If you watch a bird closely, he will tell you his story. One of spring lightness of being as he patiently gathers lint and twigs to fortify the family nest. Or one of fall urgency as he prepares for his long, arduous journey to warmer climes.

A great many people appear to be wide-open books, sharing skillfully crafted and curated life stories. However, their true motivations are hidden in cleverly concealed text; their covers and quotes merely hinting of the true story within.

The gift of the Enneagram Typology is recognizing that nine very different stories/voices, when combined, can, at their acme, produce a beautiful melody. With this sentiment, I choose to close with a quote by James Baldwin from his landmark essay "Letter from a Region in My Mind," published over sixty years ago, two years before the 1964 Civil Rights Act was signed into law: "Love takes off the masks that we fear we cannot live without and know we cannot live within."

I find this quote prophetic not only as it relates to the journey of the Enneagram but as it relates to *Being on the Wing*—navigating the joys and challenges of a life fully lived. Baldwin's mindful insight is as relevant today as it was when he wrote this quote on the page. Love, for Baldwin, is a letting go of fear—not only personal fear but fears that permeate our communities and our world.

He further writes, "I use the word 'love' (here) not merely in the personal sense but as a state of being, or a state of grace. In the tough and universal sense of quest and daring and growth." In this spirit I invite you, with great passion, grace, courage, and love—to take to the sky and enjoy *being on the wing*.

Permission to Fly

Perched for so long on this precipice,
Waiting for permission to fly
Given reasons as to why it is not yet time
The winds of change sing to my heart in a language;
With an understanding deeper and more profound
Than the deepest depths of any spoken word.
Labels that turned into sentences, paragraphs,
stories, false realities
Are falling away; freely floating to the earth as I fly higher
Towards the truth of my sun.
My purpose arrives with more clarity
with each passing moment.
It is time to celebrate
Who I am
Who you are
As we are.
Tara Becky Eschenroeder, "Landing Home"

APPENDIX I

POPULAR BIRD IDIOMS
AND RESPONSES BY TYPE

IDIOM	TYPE	RESPONSE
Get your ducks in a row	1	"Oh, please, I need to get everyone's ducks in a row!"
Charm the birds from the trees	2	"Aww. Birdies love me and I love them!"
Hit two birds with one stone	3	"Am I efficient or what?"
A rare bird	4	"Of course I am; about time you noticed!"
A bird's-eye view	5	"I see you, but you don't see me!"
A little bird told me	6	"Exactly 'which' little bird told you?"
Free as a bird	7	"Woohoo! Yippee! I'm outta here!"
Eat crow	8	"I will NOT. *You* eat crow!"
Ruffle someone's feathers	9	"Not happening."

APPENDIX II

A BIRD IN THE HAND IS
WORTH TWO IN THE BUSH

TYPE	ADAPTATION OF THE OLD ENGLISH PROVERB
1	The bird in the hand is quietly angry and thinks it would be better if all birds were in the bush.
2	The bird in the hand asks if he can lend his hand to both birds in the bush.
3	The bird in the hand considers pursuing a strategic partnership with both birds in the bush.
4	The bird in the hand longs to be free like both of the birds in the bush.
5	The bird in the hand does not chirp—as all birds are silently observing and gathering information.
6	The bird in the hand wonders why there are two birds in the bush and keeps an eye on them.
7	All of the birds are going to fly away when the going gets tough.
8	The bird in the hand wants nothing to do with the birds in the bush or this ridiculous proverb.
9	The bird in the hand is happy to join the birds in the bush or stay in the hand or they can consider other options.

BIRD SONGS: WINGED MIGRATION MESSAGES FOR EACH SUBTYPE

Type/ Subtype	Song (click for lyrics)	Artist	Migrate to
Type One	Bird Set Free	Sia	Imperfection
SP	Canary in a Coalmine	The Police	Tranquility
Soc	Bird Song	Wailin' Jennys	Joy
1:1	Rockin' Robin	Michael Jackson	Liveliness
Type Two	Song Bird	Fleetwood Mac	Unconditional Love
SP	Skyline Pigeon	Elton John	Self-sufficiency
Soc	Solsbury Hill	Peter Gabriel	Power
1:1	Catch & Release	Matt Simons	Authenticity
Type Three	Early Bird	The Eagles	Relaxation
SP	Edge of Seventeen (White-Winged Dove)	Stevie Nicks	Interdependence
Soc	Sweet Bird	Joni Mitchell	Humility
1:1	Wind Beneath My Wings	Bette Midler	Autonomy
Type Four	Birdsong	Regina Spektor	Hope
SP	I'm Like a Bird	Nelly Furtado	Freedom
Soc	Blackbird	The Beatles	Self-compassion
1:1	Birdie	Avril Lavigne	Contentment
Type Five	Sparrow	Simon & Garfunkel	Generosity
SP	Bird Song	Grateful Dead	Sharing
Soc	Norwegian Wood (This Bird Has Flown)	The Beatles	Simplicity
1:1	Gulf Coast Highway	Nancy Griffith	Familiarity

Type Six	Arlington	Wailin' Jennys	Calm
SP	Feeling Good	Cy Grant	Lightness of Being
Soc	Three Little Birds	Bob Marley and The Wailers	Pluck
1:1	Cuckoo Bird Song	Kelly Harrell	Predictability
Type Seven	Stairway to Heaven	Led Zeppelin	Reason
SP	Come Back to Me	Brandy Clark	Loyalty
Soc	Daydream Believer	Monkees	Mindfulness
1:1	I Am Not Who I Was	Chance Pena	Reality
Type Eight	Aloft	Laurie Anderson	Deep Feelings
SP	You and Me on the Rock	Brandi Carlile	Dependence
Soc	Caged Bird	Alicia Keys	Beauty
1:1	Fly Like an Eagle	Steve Miller Band	Growth
Type Nine	Take Off	Laurie Anderson	Potential
SP	Two Birds	Regina Spektor	Risk
Soc	Free Bird	Lynyrd Skynyrd	Autonomy
1:1	Carolina In My Mind	James Taylor	Independence

A bird doesn't sing because it has an answer,
it sings because it has a song.
Maya Angelou

APPENDIX IV - FEATHERED ASSESSMENT KEY

If you took the Feathered Assessment quiz on page 35, this is the key; enter on the last line of this table the number of times you chose the same Type/color.

KEY What Colors Are Your Feathers? Choose only the phrases that are absolutely your feathers!	
Type 8	I am known for my tough feathers and talons.
Type 2	I am disappointed when friends don't express appreciation about what I have done for them.
Type 3	My binoculars are focused on a direction that will result in success.
Type 7	Birding is meant to be a joyful, happy experience, not sitting around to see a particular bird.
Type 5	My metaphorical binoculars are focused on gaining more and more information.
Type 6	Before I take action I am prepared and cautious.
Type 4	I am a deeply passionate person and seek birding experiences that are awe-inspiring.
Type1	My binoculars are focused on what needs improvement.
Type 9	Conflict—ugh! I prefer to choose the flight path of least resistance
Type 5	I spend a lot of time reading about various birds and migration patterns.
Type 2	I overdo and help others adjust their lenses even when my help is unsolicited.
Type 8	A good debate serves to energize me!
Type 4	When I look through the binoculars of others, it seems they always see better birds than me.
Type 1	I tend to focus what I can do better in all of my endeavors.
Type 6	I often second-guess or re-think my decisions.
Type 7	I'd much rather anticipate something than finish it.
Type 3	Birding is a hobby where I want to succeed—but not to distract me from my many goals.

Type 9	I waiver when given many choices.
Type 1	I reflect upon how I could improve my birding (and all) skills.
Type 6	Being prepared is my bottom line.
Type 3	My running script is, "What is my next accomplishment?"
Type 4	I can spend hours empathizing with a friend who is hurting.
Type 8	Don't beat around the bush—I prefer direct communication.
Type 2	I'm exhausted. I can't keep up with the needs of my flock.
Type 7	I imagine the best possible experiences and ultimate joy!
Type 5	I think of a life as a naturally evolving mystery where I am an observer.
Type 9	I tend to go along with group decisions rather than express my own desires.
Type 1	I do *not* appreciate criticism. I am already hard enough on myself.
Type 2	When I fly, I gravitate to those who need my support.
Type 4	I have a sense of the dramatic, whether in life or when birdwatching.
Type 3	I am an efficient person.
Type 6	I often think of what can go wrong when planning an outing.
Type 5	I prefer to spend much of my time alone.
Type 7	I get bored with routine.
Type 8	I make fast, gut-based decisions.
Type 9	I will work hard and may sacrifice my own agenda to support my team.
Type 1	I focus on modeling what I perceive to be, the "right" way to behave.
Type 2	My binoculars are focused on others and how they perceive me.
Type 3	I have lots of stuff going on including bird-watching.

Type 7	People take their birding and life way too seriously.
Type 5	I share my bird knowledge sparingly, mainly with those for whom I have respect.
Type 6	My binoculars are focused on any danger that lies ahead.
Type 4	I am my moods, and can experience ecstasy and sadness when birdwatching.
Type 8	I don't have much respect for people or birds that don't stand up for themselves.
Type 9	When I feel pressured, my feathers may get ruffled.

*Total #									
Type	1	2	3	4	5	6	7	8	9
*The higher the number the more likely you associate with that particular type.									

RESOURCES

Invaluable:

Chestnut, Beatrice. *The Complete Enneagram: 27 Paths to Greater Self-Knowledge*. She Writes Press, Berkeley, CA (2013).

Inspirational:

Ackerman, Jennifer. *The Genius of Birds*. Penguin Press, NY (2016).

Birkhead, Tim. *Bird Sense: What It's Like to Be a Bird*. Bloomsbury, NY (2012).

Davison, Bill. *Easy by Nature*, Podcast and Newsletter, Podcasts.apple.com, 2023.

Habig, B., Chiyo, Patrick I, Lahti, David C. *Behavioral Ecology*, vol. 28, issue 2, 01 March-April 2017, pp. 541–548; https://doi.org/10.1093/beheco/arw187, Published: February 2017.

Lamott, Anne. *Bird by Bird: Some Instructions on Writing and Life*. Knopf Doubleday, 1994.

Marzluff, J., Angell, T. *Gifts of the Crow*, Atria Books (2013).

May, Katherine. *Wintering: The Power of Rest and Retreat in Difficult Times*. Riverhead Books, NY (2020).

Recio, Belinda. *Inside Animal Hearts and Minds: Bears that Count, Goats that Surf, and Other True Stories of Animal Intelligence and Emotion*. Skyhorse Publishing, DE (2017).

Sibley, David Allen. *What It's Like to be a Bird*. Alfred A. Knopf, NY (2020).

Tallamy, Douglas W. *Nature's Best Hope: A New Approach to Conservation that Starts in Your Yard*. Timber Press, 2020.

Taylor, Barbara Brown. *An Altar in the World: A Geography of Faith*. Harper Collins, NY (2009).

Venable, G. X., Gahm, K. & Prum, R. O. "Hummingbird plumage color diversity exceeds the known gamut of all other birds." *Commun Biol* 5, 576 (2022). https://doi.org/10.1038/s42003-022-03518-2.

Vyn, Gerrit and Cornell Lab of Ornithology. *The Living Bird: 100 Years of Listening to Nature*; Chapter 1 by Scott Weidensaul. Mountaineers Books, Seattle WA (2015).

ACKNOWLEDGMENTS

Being on the Wing is a work of creative non-fiction that is scaffolded by the centuries-old wisdom of the Enneagram; it draws from my personal stories, my *feathered* reflections on life. Readers may recall my initial book in this Enneagram in Nature series, *Nine Perfect Petals: The Enneagram for Flower Gardeners*, where I explored flowers and gardens as my palette to delve into the nine Enneagram Types. In this book I attempted to transcend the void between earth and sky, using birds as a metaphor and medium to explore the twenty-seven Enneagram Subtypes. I then hewed the twenty-seven Subtype descriptions from the narrative of my own life, especially my travels. I took great liberties in rendering bird motivations as they might translate to human motivations—the key to self-/other understanding. I drew most heavily on Beatrice Chestnut's seminal work, *The Complete Enneagram: 27 Paths to Greater Self-Knowledge*. In my estimation, her awareness and description of the unique aspects of the twenty-seven Enneagram Subtypes are absolutely brilliant. I could not have written this work without her extensive study and writings.

I consulted a number of fine books and websites to delve into the behaviors of birds, including Jennifer Ackerman's amazing book, *The Genius of Birds*, and Scott Weidensaul's, *The Living Bird*, published by the ultimate source of knowledge for all of us who love birds, the Cornell Lab of Ornithology. I have listed several other wonderful sources of inspiration in my resource section.

I am grateful to the expertise of avian scholars, including those who work on behalf of birds and the organizations that support their continuing research in bird conservation and field studies, including: The American Bird Conservancy and the Cornell Lab.

I found wisdom in the works of other nature-fond writers, such as Margaret Renkl, Katherine May, as well as the contemplative and witty works of Anne Lamott.

Over the past twenty-five years, a great many people have sparked my fascination with birds, in particular Dionisio Paniagua (Nido) of Surcostours in Panama and Costa Rica; and closer to home, our friend and neighbor Andy Upshaw. Both are incredibly skilled and knowledgeable birders who inspired me with their passion.

I cannot possibly thank every beautiful bird that has graced my own migration across the globe—from the serenading euphonias of the Costa Rican cloud forest and dazzling bee-eaters of Borneo to the scarlet tanager ablaze in the tulip tree at our farm; they have filled my days with song and color; an unconditional gift of staggering proportion.

I would like to thank my editor, Mary Neighbour, an insightful Type 5 who is a wizard at editing as well as a quiet, steady counsel in all things book-related. I am in absolute awe of Ng Hui Jing, my illustrator, who brought color and shape to my feathered reflections. Thank you is just not sufficient to express my gratitude.

Appreciation to my support flock encouraging me every word-of-the-way (aka, tier-one friends), you know who you are. I am most grateful for the time and support of my early reader/reviewers, Jenny Collins and Sadye Páez. Lynn Whitener, thank you for your literary prowess and time spent on my behalf. I am so lucky to have Kathleen, of KathleenHunter photography.com as my dear friend—thank you for my author photo! To my sister, JoAnn McCaffrey, who introduced me to the Enneagram, I am forever grateful.

It goes without saying that this book series would never have been written without the support of my husband, Marty Rosenberg. He brought me to the farm in 1995—and it was love at first visit (man, dog, and farm). Marty, thank you for your unconditional support of this book. I am so privileged to nest and migrate with you by my side.

The Enneagram calls us to embrace our shadows—like birds, to fly into the billowing clouds without fear and emerge into a clear sky; on the wing, toward the light.

Angela Roseberg

ABOUT THE AUTHOR

Dr. Angela Rosenberg, DrPH, focuses on leadership development and advancement of individuals and teams through her company, Inside Out Enneagram. She is a Board Certified Leadership Coach (BCC) who uses a variety of assessment approaches in her workshops and retreats; the Enneagram is, admittedly, her favorite. She has presented and consulted on team-building approaches and strategic planning with numerous national organizations and has authored publications in several peer-reviewed journals. Angela also wrote and illustrated *The Shell and Me*, a children's book.

She enjoys birding all over the world, especially on her North Carolina farm where she lives with her husband, Great Danes, a Golden Doodle, donkeys, and one brave cat. *Being on the Wing: Feathered Reflections on the Enneagram Subtypes* is the second book in the Enneagram in Nature series. Her first book, *Nine Perfect Petals: The Enneagram for Flower Gardeners,* was an award winner, garnering praise from critics and readers. Find her series online or request it in your favorite independent bookstore.

www.ingramcontent.com/pod-product-compliance
Lightning Source LLC
Chambersburg PA
CBHW051315020426
42333CB00028B/3352